What people ~~saying~~ *Inspiraton at Work . . .*

"Dr. Robert Ruotolo's book INSPIRATION AT WORK is an insightful guide to the exploration of oneself from both a personal and a business perspective. Dr. Ruotolo has combined his personal and business experiences covering three decades to provide an aid to assist others in reaching their maximum potential. The publication is a combination of theory, experiential exercises and introspection put forward in what can only be described as an easy read. To those who wish to help others or themselves explore their potential, I recommend this guide."

Bill Rankin, B.Sc., B.Ed., M.S., C.H.R.P.
Vice President, Human Resources
Newcourt Credit Group

". . . powerful, compelling . . . the functional and original concepts of 'wealth' and being a 'co-designer of your present and future' set this work apart from other writings on the subject. A harmonious way of controlling one's own destiny."

"Being the architect of your present and future is a powerful concept and central theme. 'Wealth is an asset which brings good to others and to myself without harm or deprivation to any.' These insights and applications can change the way we live and work in the corporate world!"

Ronald Gomes
President .
Digital Consulting, Inc.

"Dr. Ruotolo's book reminds us of the important fact that organizational improvement will only happen if there are strong, centered people whose professional work is guided by the five principles that he describes. The culture and practices of an organization are only a reflection of the people within it."

Constance Bentley
President and CEO
Zenger Miller

"I've spent twenty years in and around teaching and facilitating individual growth and development. A common thread through the fabric of my work has been attempting to awaken the great potential of the human spirit and how it can be harnessed to achieve great things for one's self, community, church and business organization.

"INSPIRATION AT WORK: Igniting a New Entrepreneurial Spirit in the Individual and the Corporation provides a meaningful framework for anyone seeking more control over their life and to more strongly influence what matters most to them.

"The work is worthy of consideration by individuals and organizations seeking such an awakening and taking subsequent action."

Robert A. Brownlow

"Dr. Ruotolo shares with us, in a workshop-like format, the steps to structure a balanced life, one with direction and increased visioning.

"This book is a participative and interactive blueprint for a balanced and successful life. It reads easily while involving the reader in a personal way. Dr. Ruotolo candidly reveals how his life has been made better through awareness and application of the tools described in the book.

"Intended for anyone doing business, whether out of one's home or in the largest corporation, Dr. Ruotolo's step-by-step guide asks the right questions. Our thoughtful answers lead to a balanced and successful life.

"The author shows that one's life is not pre-determined, but rather a pathway upon which self-awareness, planning and the support of others can lead to desired results!"

Paul Kennedy
President
International Data Corporation (Canada) Ltd.

". . . can help individuals (and their partners) work through a process to greatly enhance their success and satisfaction in life."

Dr. Warren Wilhelm
Global Consulting Alliance

INSPIRATION AT WORK

Robert A. Ruotolo, D.S.W.

Inspiration *at* **Work:**

IGNITING A NEW
ENTREPRENEURIAL
SPIRIT IN THE
INDIVIDUAL
AND THE
CORPORATION

Foreword by Lennon Ledbetter

Dona Nobís Pacem Press
SCOTTDALE, ARIZONA

Cover image ©1997 PhotoDisc, Inc.

Printed in the United States of America.

10 9 8 7 6 5 4 3 2 1
First Printing 1997

ISBN 0-9651541-0-6
Library of Congress Catalog Number: 96-072560

Cover and text design by Regina Crisman.

Publisher's Cataloguing in Publication
(Prepared by Quality Books Inc.)

Ruotolo, Robert A.
      Inspiration at work: igniting a new entrepreneurial spirit in the
    individual and the corporation / Robert A. Ruotolo.
    p. cm.
    Includes bibliographical references.
    ISBN 0-9651541-0-6

      1. Entrepreneurship. 2. Organizational change. 3. Self-actualization
(Psychology) 4. Spiritual life. I. Title.

HB615.R86 1997   338.04
                                        QBI96-40850

This book is dedicated to my wife, Patricia,

and my three daughters,

Kymberly, Kara-Lee, and Kinsey-Beth.

Each has been an inspiration to me in a different way

throughout the writing

and the living of this work.

TABLE OF
CONTENTS

ACKNOWLEDGMENTS

MANY HAVE CONTRIBUTED over the years to what has eventually resulted in the written form of this book.

Of course, my family, friends and colleagues have continually provided the environment and support necessary to persevere in such a task. However, it is important that I acknowledge by name a number of individuals who have contributed to the success of this project: Dr. Susan Corso, editor, publication project manager and friend — her continued advice and positive spirit energized me; reviewers Connie Bentley, Robert Brownlow, Ron Gomes, Paul Kennedy, Lennon Ledbetter, Don Redlinger and Warren Wilhelm gave their comments and responses with enthusiasm.

A special thanks goes to Louise and Gregory Corbett for actually going through every exercise and providing me valuable feedback on their effectiveness; in addition, their continued encouragement and positive regard for my work and effort kept me going.

AlliedSignal Aerospace has enabled me to practice my work within its organization and has provided me richness in experience and support. The Ahwatukee Toastmasters afforded me the opportunity for creative speechwriting that spawned the genesis of many of the ideas and concepts in the text.

FOREWORD

I AM SO EXCITED about what Dr. Bob Ruotolo
has to say to all of us, whether we are corporate leaders,
employees, entrepreneurs in our own businesses, or any other
roles we may play in life! In INSPIRATION AT WORK, he
is sharing with us the fundamentals of how to be a Success
(with a capital S) and how to live a fuller life. As we journey
through this experience called living, we need practical guide-
posts. Dr. Bob Ruotolo's INSPIRATION AT WORK:
Igniting a New Entrepreneurial Spirit in the Individual and
the Corporation gives invaluable insights that serve us well.

Today individuals, entrepreneurs, and corporate leaders are being challenged with how to create wealth without
sacrificing the human side of enterprise. Dr. Ruotolo provides
us with a process-oriented model that enables individuals to
grow, teams to explode, and everyone to profit beyond economics both inside and outside of the corporate context. The
author's emphasis on being process-oriented, not just end
result-oriented, is an important key to happiness and a sense
of well-being. Success is a process; goal-setting is a process;
the value of both lies not only in achievement, but also in a
sense of direction for one's life.

In a time when people are compartmentalizing life
and then specializing in one compartment at the expense of
the others, his ideas on developing the whole person, on
having a balanced life, and on becoming a total being are

refreshing. Dr. Ruotolo reminds us of the important role basic beliefs and core values play in guiding our goal choices and behaviors. A person's goal choices and behavior are the expression of basic beliefs and core values. Strategic models and skills that have been the prerogative of senior management and executives for years are made available and recognized as critical to all individuals.

Dr. Ruotolo states the principles and practices that our organization has followed over the years to assure both individual and corporate success. The ongoing growth and development of the individual is paramount! The need for a sense of ownership and a strong team spirit are equally vital! Individuals grow, teams explode! There is a synergistic power in INSPIRATION AT WORK. The importance of being able to create your own dreams to ignite and fuel your performance cannot be underestimated. The ongoing need for positive mental conditioning and the know-how to do it are well demonstrated.

Dr. Ruotolo's thirty years of experience as a family therapist, sports psychologist, and organization consultant bring to us a profound understanding and teaching of how to create environments in which we can grow and prosper together. In a day when so many people are looking externally for justification, Dr. Bob Ruotolo declares, "You get to take responsibility for who and what you are!" His words set up an echo within us that literally creates inspiration at work, at play, in life. Reading this book is a must!

Lennon Ledbetter
Executive Diamond
Amway Corporation

• PART I •
The Five Basic Principles:
Blueprint for Success

INTRODUCTION

THICH NHAT HANH, a Vietnamese Buddhist monk, nominated for the Nobel Peace Prize by Martin Luther King, Jr., wrote:

> *"We can smile, breathe, walk, and eat our meals in a way that allows us to be in touch with the abundance of happiness that is available. We are very good at preparing to live, but not very good at living. We know how to sacrifice ten years for a diploma, and we are willing to work very hard to get a job, a car, a house, and so on. But we have difficulty remembering that we are alive in the present moment, the only moment there is for us to be alive . . . ."*

Each of us touches our reality, that awareness of living in the moment, at various times in our lives. It is almost always unexpected and frequently a shattering of something old and a bridge to something new. Should this be so? Is it possible if we learn the means to knowing ourselves on all of our possible levels that we will also learn to live fully in each moment?

Recently I began my work day at a 7 AM meeting with a project team preparing a "Quest for Excellence" competition. The meeting went really well! I was excited and pumped at the start of a new day. Running a few minutes behind, I called my office and left a voice-mail message that I was on my way to my appointment with my colleague Bob.

When I arrived Sara, my assistant, anxiously told me that another colleague, Dave, had been rushed to the hospital with a heart attack! My meeting was cancelled. Bob and some of my other co-workers were at the hospital. I decided to go there, too.

There I was, confronting the moment, asking myself questions, like should I go to the hospital? What about all my work? What can I do when I get there? Could this happen to me? When I saw the frightened faces of Dave's wife and their children, I thought, what if it were my wife, Pat? My emotions ran rampant as I tried to comfort Dave's family, speak with my co-workers, and confront the echo in my soul.

This is reality. This is living in the moment. This is as much a part of life as the daily routine of home, family, work, play and faith. I take all those parts of my life for granted. Don't you? Do you have to be confronted with a dramatic event to recognize that you are alive? This moment you are alive! Are YOU truly alive?

Dave did recover. He has never been able to return to work and has had to change the way he functions in his daily routine of living. However, he does know that he is alive in the moment. His experience and my participation in it is one of the reasons I feel compelled to share with you the knowledge that ignites a new entrepreneurial spirit in the individual and the corporation. Such a spirit gives you the abilities to live a fuller life in the present and still prepare for the challenges ahead, the abilities to foster a desire to be creative and to lead change — to be the 'architect/designer' of our present and future, to build these needed capabilities not only in ourselves, but also into the businesses and organizations of which we are a part.

The new entrepreneurial spirit is self-directed; fosters a sense of ownership and partnership; focuses on health and wealth creation, on wholeness, on inclusion; is principle-centered.

Working in the free world today has become confusing and anxiety-filled. I call it, affectionately, *organizational madness*. I find when I give something a name it helps me begin to understand it. We are challenged today with all the parts of that madness: down-sizing, right-sizing, mergers, acquisitions and closures. We go from paychecks to copiers to virtual reality to pink slips. We have employment contracts.

I remember when one was hired by a company and stayed with them all one's life. One received a gold watch on retirement and a monthly check for the rest of one's life. No more. Each worker is required to have a contract, and upgrade his or her skills on a continuing basis in order to keep the job and reach successive levels. Each time one learns a new technology, a newer one emerges. Businesses and the work they produce easily relocate geographically. It's not so easy for the worker anymore. Without achieving these types of goals, the pink slip is very nearly inevitable.

We all need to rethink the roles we live, our relationships and our life expectations. We need to stop compartmentalizing and start integrating our lives. We need to examine our relationships with our partners, with our families, our employers, our employees and with ourselves. It is the whole person that is the future of the world. It is the whole person, as he or she learns the tools of self-management and puts them into practice in the moment, that will lead the world to thrive in peace. It is the concept of self-management as defined in this text which leads to new entrepreneurial behaviors in the individual and the corporation.

This book was written to guide you through a process of self-assessment. You are provided with five principles from which you can draw vibrance and reverence for your life. They take into consideration the human condition, life's hindrances and obstacles, and lead you to a compatible understanding of your life. The five principles are appropriate as a guide for you as an individual, and for you in relationship to a spouse or partner, friend or co-worker. These principles apply as well to organizational units like families, work groups, teams and organizations as a whole.

Principle I: I Know Myself.

Do you? I will guide you through the process of exploring your value and belief systems as part of establishing a framework for goal-setting for the whole you. This same guided process can be applied to your organization, to enable it to become "a learning organization," thus giving it a competitive edge.

Principle II: I Establish a Personal Set of Values and Beliefs.

Elie Weisel says, " . . . when our center is strong, everything else is secondary . . . ."

Values create beliefs, and beliefs create behavior. We'll work on it together.

Principle III: I Take Responsibility for Who and What I Am.

Only you are responsible for who you are and who you want to be. This fosters both self-sufficiency and harmony with others.

Principle IV: I Am a Co-designer of My Life, Who I Am and Who I Want to Become.

Remember organizational madness? Is it possible to self-manage your own career even if your organization is re-engineering? I think so. You can learn the means to sculpting a better and more meaningful life at work, at home and at play.

Principle V: I Celebrate the Present and Give Thanks.

The breath of life is the present. We walk together in celebration of your achievements and of your life. We need to appreciate and recognize one another.

These principles should guide and reinforce you to behave in a way that will lead to self-discovery, vision, a sense of purpose, core personal and organizational values, commitment, creativity, and adaptability.

In preparation for the exploration upon which we are to embark together, I will share some of my own horror stories so that you know that I began where you may be, and that I live on the continuum learned from the principles and the way to achieve them that I now share with you.

The journey which ignites your new entrepreneurial spirit and that of the corporation is one of inspiration.

Inspiration allows you to examine the past, live in the present to the fullest degree and be the architect of your future. The disciplines that we are about to explore will provide the tools for you and your organization's future. **This is Inspiration at Work.**

PRINCIPLE I:
I KNOW MYSELF

Be more concerned with your character than your reputation, because your character is what you really are, while your reputation is merely what others think you are.

John Wooden
UCLA Head Basketball Coach

We live out our past oftentimes, we limit our perspective to past references, citing the evidence of yesterday as proof of what is possible. But evidence tells us nothing about what we can be and do if we choose to walk a different path.

B. N. Kaufman

Everyone has a purpose in Life — a unique gift or talent . . . and when we blend this unique talent with service to others, we experience the ecstasy and exultation of all goals.

Deepak Chopra
The Seven Spiritual Laws of Success

WHAT IS SELF-KNOWLEDGE?
It is an awareness of who you are in the context of where
you exist. You play many roles in and through your life.
Each one is a manifestation of who you are, as you see yourself and as others see you. It is an opportunity for constant
and ongoing discovery.

Self-knowledge is a life-long process. It begins in your
formative, early childhood years, when you first learn to
interpret feedback from yourself and from others. That feedback was either positive, negative or a mixture of both. It is
this element that begins to form your attitude about yourself,
your self-perception.

The roots of your self-image and self-esteem are
formed in your early years. Self-image is two-fold: how you
see yourself and how you believe others see you. Self-esteem
is the degree to which you value yourself as a person. You
may also define your self-esteem within the parameters of a
group, a team, an organization or institution.

Does your self-knowledge ever fail you? Yes. Self-
knowledge fails you and keeps you from fulfilling your potential when it is not supported by a positive attitude and a positive set of beliefs about yourself and the world around you.
It fails you when there is a loss of faith and hope about your
existence. Your first insights to your successes and failures
begin with the *dos* and *don'ts* of early childhood. *"You're a
good boy," "That was very good"* or *"What a naughty girl,"*
begin to form your values and beliefs about yourself as a person and your place in society. You begin to determine what
is good for you to think or do or say and what is bad for you

to think or do or say by the reactions of the people around you: parents, relatives, caregivers and others in roles of authority and influence.

As you study the model, **14 Dimensions of Diversity,** you will understand how complex it is to discover who you are and from whence you come.

1 4   D I M E N S I O N S   O F   D I V E R S I T Y

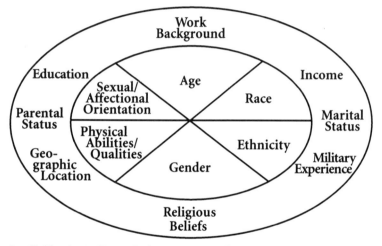

From *Workforce America, Managing Employee Diversity as a Vital Resource.*
M. Loden and J. Rosener, Irwin, 1991.

In this model the word *dimension* refers to the properties and characteristics that constitute the whole person. These dimensions are further broken down into two categories, primary (inner circle) and secondary (outer circle).

The primary properties and characteristics are central to your identity. They are immutable and salient. They are present at birth and have significant impact on how you were socialized as a child. They shape your self-image and world view. Others make judgments about you based on their assumptions of these dimensions.

The secondary dimensions are characteristics that you acquire and can modify. Their presence or absence does not change your core identity. They add another layer to your self-definition.

As you gain in life experiences, you begin to evaluate these former, usually unconscious, judgments you have formulated about yourself and the world around you. Based on this new information, and with improved mental capabilities to process the information, you will either affirm or alter your earlier perceptions. This requires a condition called *openness of mind*.

It takes a conscious effort to challenge your perceptions or beliefs. This consciousness is prompted by some inner or outer stimulus. Something from within tells you that your normal response to a particular situation does not fit.

I refer to this process as *mental conditioning*.

I worked as a sports psychologist with the competitive swimmers for the 1984 Canadian Olympic trials. I focused on the mental attitude of every individual performer in order to better prepare them for their event. I found that it was here, in the mental arena of the athlete's mind, that the quality of the performance was determined. Together we fostered mental preparedness through positive imagery.

Each athlete would experience repetitive mental rehearsals, visualizing a complete performance from prerace, the race itself and the celebration of victory. They learned how to manage their energy levels through relaxation exercises and energizing activity. The swimmers learned to focus before and during competition. They learned to block out all extraneous distractions, within and without, including their competition in the next lane and the fears and anxieties that might surface from within.

Mental Conditioning is

a gradual, life-long process which includes both internal and external feedback;

the manner in which our thoughts, attitudes and beliefs about ourselves, others and the world around us evolve;

how we interpret messages from within and outside ourselves in order to determine who and what we are.

Mental conditioning is a powerful capability of humankind. This power enables us to transform ourselves, like a sculptor who molds a beautiful work of art from a ball of clay or an awesome figure from a block of granite.

You are the sculptor of your life. When thinking of your life in terms of clay, you work with gentle fingertips, smoothing and soothing the material to your desired result. If you were to think of this process from the point of view of the stone sculptor, you would use a chisel and a mallet, striking the stone and chipping it away, again and again, until you achieved your desired result.

Sometimes life's continuum of transformation is soft and smooth, while at other times it is rife with pain and sharpness. Both modes are appropriate in the hands of a loving craftsman. Both modes are able to transform an object into something of beauty. Each method is dependent on the vision, beliefs, skills and the desire of the artist.

Mental conditioning is the instrument by which you can respond to the past and act in the present, so that you may prepare for the future! It is a critical skill to transform and change yourself, to respond to and influence the world around you. It is through this mental conditioning process that your self-image is shaped and reinforced. This same mental conditioning process works as successfully for groups, work teams and organizations as for the individual. In the workplace, a more familiar name for the process is *culture change*.

In your role as leader, be it teacher, parent, team leader, manager, coach or politician, you will have an impact on the mental conditioning of those you lead. When you as a leader are truly alive, that conditioning process will be positive.

An example of the mental impact of environment on a child follows:

Children Learn What They Live

If a child lives with criticism,
    He learns to condemn.
If a child lives with hostility,
    She learns to fight.
If a child lives with ridicule,
    He learns to be shy.
If a child lives with shame,
    She learns to feel guilty.
If a child lives with tolerance,
    He learns to be patient.
If a child lives with encouragement,
    She learns confidence.
If a child lives with praise,
    He learns to appreciate.
If a child lives with fairness,
    She learns justice.
If a child lives with security,
    He learns to have faith.
If a child lives with approval,
    She learns to like herself.
If children live with acceptance
and friendship,
    They learn to find love in
the world.

Dorothy Law Nolte
(my paraphrase)

Now try this self-assessment instrument that will assist you in evaluating the mental conditioning processes that currently exist within your organization. Use this to rate your organization and to establish an action plan in those areas that need improvement.

How does your leadership and organization rate on a scale of one to ten, ten being excellent?

A Mental Conditioning Self-Assessment Questionnaire

1. Symbols: purpose, vision, values, beliefs.

_____

What symbols do you have and use that communicate who you are as a member of your organization and what do you believe in as a business entity about yourself and why the organization exists?

2. Systems and structure.   _____

How is your organization structured? Does it have levels? How is it staffed? How is it organized? Are there rewards and recognition systems in place? Do they work?

3. Valuing your employees.   _____

What messages does the leadership communicate to the employees about themselves, their performance and their relative position in the organization? How do these messages affect the employees' self-image?

4. Leadership behaviors and role modeling. _____

How does your behavior and that of the managers affect the mental conditioning of the employees? What are you and the managers like as role models? What are your strengths as a role model? What are your limitations as a role model?

5. Developing others. _____

What approach to training employees do you use? Do you give and encourage immediate feedback? Do you foster mentoring on the job? Do you set up job assignments for this purpose? Do you assure direct and immediate job application of new skills acquired from off-the-job training?

6. Roles and responsibilities. _____

How do you handle relationships with employees? Do you carefully define each person's role? Do you establish mutual expectations?

7. Rewards and recognition. _____

What techniques do you use to foster a positive mental attitude with an employee? Do you use peer and team performance awards? Do you implement informal praise?

8. Methods and techniques in positive mental conditioning. _____

Are you knowledgeable and skillful in the application of current methods in mental conditioning? Are you effectively and systematically designing these methods into your current employees' development programs? Are you using TQ tools, visualization techniques and positive imagery?

How did you score yourself on this mini assessment?

_____

This capability to transform yourself and to work with others in this process will be gained and supported by the process you will find in **Inspiration At Work** and its related works. The process of transforming your self comes from both internal and external feedback, through your relationships within and without.

To Know Yourself requires a range of self-knowledge. It requires understanding your nature and the human condition. This is why it is a lifetime continuum. We learn in many ways: intellectually, experientially, through our senses, by observation and reflection. The following model illustrates self-knowledge in the Whole Person.

THE WHOLE PERSON

Mind	Body	Spirit
• Intellectual/ Rational • Creative • Innovative • Emotional/ Attitudinal	• Weight/Diet • Endurance/Stamina • Organ Function	• Sense of Purpose/ Meaningfulness • Transcendence/ Connectedness • Mystical/ Metaphysical

Well-Being

• Physical
• Psychological
• Social
• Spiritual

• Where do you stand in the realm of well-being?

• Are you sacrificing one thing for another?

• Do you have balance and harmony between each realm of your being?

• Do you have a sense of vibrancy in your life?

If your answers are yes, you may want to follow along to affirm what you are doing to maintain this level of being truly alive. If your answers are no, you may wish to explore how to move to a more balanced lifestyle.

Life is full of twists and turns, many that we least expect. It is the journey of humankind. We come into this world as unique individuals, but with basically the same human nature. We all leave this life in the same way, our material and temporal belongings forgotten. It is what we do with our lives while we are on earth that makes the quality of our existence!

I will guide you through the process of exploring your value and belief system as part of establishing a framework for goal-setting. Here you will have an opportunity to assess your current values and to decide whether or not your values will take you where you want to be!

PRINCIPLE II:
I ESTABLISH
A PERSONAL SET
OF VALUES AND BELIEFS

*First we must understand that there can be
no life without risk — and when our center
is strong, everything else is secondary, even
the risks. Thus, we best prepare by building
our inner strength, by sound philosophy, by
reaching out to others, by asking ourselves
what matters most.*

Elie Wiesel
Nobel Peace Prize Laureate
Holocaust survivor

- What is really important to you?
- If you were to look back at your life, what would you want said about your life and the way you led it?
- What would you be most proud of?
- What would you be least proud of?

You have probably already started to answer these questions.

- Do you like what you see?
- Do you like what you hear?
- Who are your associates?
- Are you affiliated with an organization?

You can positively influence the answers to these questions. You cannot change the past, but you can change the present. The present is the only time you can effect a change. You can work on it. It is your decision to make. Make it now!

Take a few moments and reflect on the above questions and answers.

- What do your reflections say about your intrinsic values?

Intrinsic values are those which actually guide and direct your decisions and behaviors. Stated values are derived and conditioned from outside influences such as your social relationships, your place of worship, or your workplace. It is frequently assumed that your stated values are the ones that guide your decisions and behaviors. This is not necessarily the case.

• What does your actual behavior say about your values?

• What is the difference between what is good for you and what you perceive to be good for you?

• What does your behavior say about making choices between short-term good and long-term good?

• Do you have the ability to defer pleasure?

• Do you have prejudices?

• Are any of these things in conflict with your values?

Understanding your responses to the above questions can help you work through a values clarification exercise. This will enable you to learn what are *your* true values and beliefs. You will have a greater consciousness of the relationship between your actual behavior and your true values and a better awareness of the inner conflicts you experience from time to time. These conflicts are natural and are usually associated with a hierarchy of values and preferences.

Your personal value system consists of three components; values create beliefs, and beliefs create behaviors. Your values provide direction for your beliefs.

For instance, one of your core values may be integrity. Your value informs your belief. Your belief is your interpretation of how you will act out your value of integrity in a personal or social context. Your beliefs about integrity may be to be honest with yourself and others about how you think and feel about something or someone, to be genuine, to be open. This is a behavioral attribute which you and others associate with integrity. Your behavior may consist of sharing your thoughts and feelings in regard to a particular situation. If an action is required as a result of your belief, it would be accomplished in a manner that is consistent and appropriate to your value structure.

It is important to keep in mind as you identify and assess your current set of values, that they span over all the key areas of your life that contribute to your wellbeing: physical, social, emotional, mental and spiritual. Drawing from each segment creates balance in your life. Your value structure transforms as you mature, especially if you approach it deliberately and consciously. You need to strive for congruence between your values, beliefs and behaviors. When this congruence does not exist, inner tension and negative stress will manifest itself in some form, physically or emotionally.

In my private practice, I consulted with a regional office of a national insurance company and spoke to some of its management personnel. In our discussions about the company and how it conducts business they shared the following story.

A prospective employee may ask, "Why does this company care what my values are? If I have the level of knowledge and intelligence to do an outstanding job, why do they ask me to identify and understand my values?"

The reason is because neither knowledge nor intelligence is enough. The kind of judgments this employee will have to make about the way to use her abilities is related to her values. *How to* is technical knowledge. *What to* is philosophical. *What to* knowledge is directed by values and gives direction to our lives and to the organizations for which we work.

The test of our personal philosophy is the effectiveness of our decisions and the excellence of our performance. The test of our company philosophy is the commercial marketplace. There our philosophy must be proven by effective service.

Many companies go through the exercise of creating a Value Statement which is prominently displayed on the office wall. The value of the statement is only as effective as the understanding, acceptance and action of the employees in their day-to-day behavior with each other, their customers and their suppliers.

While on a consulting assignment for an international oil company, I was asked to visit a number of their sites to interview both management and union personnel in order to assess the relationship between the two. During a session with union representatives, I observed that there was tension regarding their relationship with management.

I saw a statement of company beliefs hanging on the wall. I asked the representatives to read the statement to me and share with me their opinion of it. Their response was, "Management brought in a consultant, put a committee together to make it up, and spent $250,000!" They felt no ownership for what was written on the plaque. They could not identify with it nor did they see the beliefs as an integral part of management behavior.

We spent the next thirty minutes working on how to use the Belief Statement as a tool with management to jointly define mutually agreed upon behavior that reflected it. I later met with management, explained what I had observed, and what I had facilitated so that union and management could work together effectively.

It is this kind of interaction that is needed to make your beliefs come alive in your day-to-day existence with the people with whom you live and work.

In one of my workshops entitled, "Creating New Mental Software," I use the metaphor of the brain as a personal computer and the mind as software. I speak of the power of beliefs. Beliefs produce life experiences, not the other way around. Your beliefs interpret your reality. Your beliefs about yourself, your capabilities, your self-image, all affect how you will respond in any given situation. Your beliefs about others such as bias, prejudice, stereotypes, likes and dislikes, all impact your first impression of someone else. Just think how profound a difference it makes to your perspective on life around you and your behavior if you have an abundance mentality instead of a scarcity mentality. With an abundance mentality, you believe there is plenty for everyone. When you have a scarcity mentality, you believe that there is not enough to go around so you better get yours first!

Knowing and challenging your value and belief system is important to your self-image. How you think and feel about yourself and your social functioning is an important part of being truly alive. Peter Senge in his text, **The Fifth Discipline,** conveys the power of beliefs through the Ladder of Inference.

THE LADDER OF INFERENCE

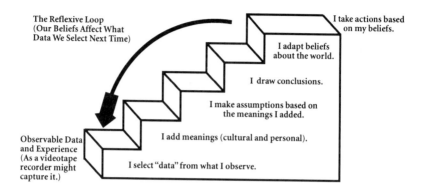

The Reflexive Loop
(Our Beliefs Affect What
Data We Select Next Time)

I take actions based on my beliefs.

I adapt beliefs about the world.

I draw conclusions.

I make assumptions based on the meanings I added.

Observable Data and Experience (As a videotape recorder might capture it.)

I add meanings (cultural and personal).

I select "data" from what I observe.

The following story illustrates this Ladder of Inference.

A man was phoning a home. A young child answered the phone. "Hello," said the child in a whisper. The man asked, "Is there an adult at home?" and the child replied in a whisper, "Yes, my mommy is home, but she's busy."

What are you thinking as the story unfolds? What inferences have you made based on the data that you have? Write down your thoughts and assumptions at this point.

The man on the phone asks, "Is there anyone else at home?" The child replies, "Yes, my daddy is at home." "May I speak to him?" the man asks. "No," the child replies, "he's busy, too."

With this added information, what are you thinking now? Write down your conclusions.

The man continues to inquire, "Is there anyone else at home?" "Yes," the child says in a
whisper, "there is a policeman with my parents." "Is there anyone else there?" the man
asks in a perplexed voice. "Yes," the child
replies, "a fireman."

What have you concluded now? Have your initial
suppositions changed with more information? How have
your beliefs about this kind of situation colored your interpretation of what is going on? Isn't this how we proceed
throughout each day as life unfolds before us?

After some hesitation the man asks the child,
"Why are you whispering?" The child
replies, "Because they are all looking for me!"

What are your thoughts now? Is this child a boy or
a girl? Were you surprised by the ending? Were you
surprised with how and why your thoughts changed as the
story progressed?

Later in Part II of this text, I will guide you through a
process to explore your value and belief system as part of a
framework for goal-setting. There you will have an opportunity to assess your current values and beliefs and decide
whether they will take you where you want to be!

PRINCIPLE III:
I TAKE RESPONSIBILITY
FOR WHO AND WHAT I AM

Ultimately, man should not ask what the meaning to life is, but rather must recognize that it is he who is asked. In a word, each man is questioned by life; and he can only answer to life by answering for his own life; to life he can only respond by being responsible.

Viktor Frankl

TAKING RESPONSIBILITY for who and what you are naturally follows the ideas we have discussed in the first two principles. In conjunction with knowing yourself and the key values that guide you to fulfillment, you can be inner-directed regarding what actions you take in any given situation.

You are responsible and accountable for your actions. I am being specific here regarding the term *action* rather than *thought*. However, you are also responsible for your deliberate thoughts which ultimately lead to your behavior. These patterns can become habits of thought that later will govern how you respond. This is how you program yourself.

It is important to reflect occasionally on who you are and what you do, to assess the appropriateness of your behavior in relationship to yourself and the other people in your life. Ask yourself these questions.

• Am I the person I want to be?

• Is my behavior in accordance with my value and belief system?

• Am I fostering the kind of relationships with myself and with others that I choose?

These questions and their answers can be your rallying point. You may decide to hold fast to your existing values, beliefs and behaviors or an alarm may sound which tells you to try something different.

• Is your behavior having the effect you desire?

Many times what you do or say is subtly affected by what you think. You do not always realize the impact your thought or outside exposure has on your behavior. An example is when a story, told over and over again by the media, begins to threaten your personal and physical security. The media can build in or foster certain biases and attitudes.

Recently there was a terrible bombing of a government building in one of our major cities. The initial media response was speculation about a foreign terrorist at work. Some suspects were taken into custody.

Often our first response is to look for the enemy "out there." We notice differences in others and make them wrong.

In the particular situation I am citing, the difference was more subtle: it was a difference of values. The individual charged was an American citizen but he did not believe in what his government was doing. Further, he believed he had the right to take the lives of many who were in the building at the time of the explosion.

Daily reality does seem to be getting more drastic, and more dramatic. And the media play it for all it's worth. Bad news sells, not good news. People are becoming more and more concerned with their personal security and that of their loved ones. We are internalizing these messages of danger. They are affecting how we think and what we do.

However, we need to remember that we have the ability to choose. We do not have to play

the victim to disasters or the media or any-
thing else. I believe we have an obligation to
choose the positive path toward constructive
thought and action. This contributes, in
a greater sense, to making the world a
better place.

There is a saying in the computer world that is appropriate here. *Garbage in, garbage out. Good stuff in, good
stuff out.* What kind of programming are you allowing by
what you hear and watch? What do you read and for what
purpose? Are you positively or negatively reinforcing
thoughts, attitudes and behaviors that are important to your
well-being?

This is **HEAVY STUFF!** You do not realize at times
the control and influence that you give up to outside sources
which slowly erode the power you have over who you are or
what you want to be. You need to empower yourself! Once
you become conscious of what is happening to you and to
your mind, you can take more positive control of your own
destiny. This is an unfolding process with more and more
"Ahas" each day.

Recently returning from a business trip, I
knew I was tired and was looking forward to
getting home.

At the airport, while waiting for the shuttle
to take me to my car, I saw a gentleman
approaching selling newspapers to earn
money for a night's lodging. I had seen this
man at the same place on previous trips.
I was not in a very charitable mood and did
not want to engage in conversation. I tried to
avoid eye contact with him. You know how
that goes.

However, he did approach me in a polite, friendly, engaging manner with some helpful inquiring comments. "Good evening, did you have a good trip? Do you need help with directions?" I kept my distance with half-engaging comments. "Are you waiting for a van?" he asked. I said, "Yes, Park and Fly." He said, "You mean Park 'n Travel." He was right! I said, "Sometimes I mix up the name. I go to the south side rather than the north side for pick up." He pointed at the blue sign and said, "You see where it says North on the sign?" At first, I truly did not see it. He repeated himself and then I did see it for the first time in all my travels. Right there on the sign, **North!** In the future I would have no reason to confuse the north side of the terminal with the south.

Then he asked if I wanted to make a donation for a paper and he explained why. No pressure. He was very polite. He was well-spoken and evidently bright. All I had was some small change which I gave to him in exchange for the paper. I was somewhat apologetic, but he made me feel very comfortable. Earlier in our encounter, while I was distancing myself, he made a comment to me that did not strike me until later when I was reflecting on the whole incident. He said, "Your behavior towards me is more a reflection of you as a person than who I am."

He was absolutely right! My stereotyping and prejudice was coming out all over.

Remember the proverb, "What you do to the
least of my people you do unto me." I learned
a lot from that gentleman about myself in a
very short period of time.

Sometimes you may separate what you think and feel
and how you act spiritually from what you think, feel and
how you act socially. You will discover ambivalence, mixed
feelings, as you begin to break down the walls inside yourself
by clarifying your own value structure.

We all create convenient silos. You may say within
certain situations a given behavior is fine. When I am with
the boys, it's alright to tell off-color jokes and use certain lan-
guage but it is not acceptable in mixed company. You may
want to rethink that set of behaviors and ask yourself, "How
does this behavior set contribute to the betterment of what I
am doing and who I want to be?"

Often people separate their work world from
their personal life. John, a thirty-two year old
homebuilder/developer, has a young family
with his wife, Betty. John and Betty are active
in their community and church.

John describes his industry as a "dog-eat-dog
world." "You always have to watch your
back." His self-talk is painful. "With the
cycles in this business, you could lose everything overnight." John says he's had to work
hard for everything he's gotten; nothing has
come easy. I'm sure you get the idea.

When John comes home, he steps out of his
work role and relaxes with his wife and two
preschool-age children. Betty spends most of
her time caring for the boy and girl, and

works part-time as a court stenographer. John is a caring husband and father; he shows empathy with his wife and children.

What are some of the possible conflicts that could arise with John as time goes on? What will he teach his children about work? About competition? Will John be successful long-term? What kind of mental pressures is he likely to experience?

You will find many similar examples when you rewrite your inner rule book. There are consequences to these changes and sometimes they are difficult to assimilate. You have established expectations around your existing behavior patterns with others. They may not wish to see you change. It is not easy to challenge a norm already set. It is not easy to be the role model for change.

However, there are ways that you can positively influence others to help you succeed in changing your behavior and to continue to build on your existing relationship. There may be times when you have to take a stand and decide to change regardless of the consequences. You may even decide to leave a relationship because you have outgrown it. These changes should not be taken lightly. They are a challenge, but you can do it! You are responsible for who you are and who you want to be.

PRINCIPLE IV:
I AM A CO-DESIGNER
OF MY LIFE,
WHO I AM AND
WHO I WANT TO BECOME

You the coach, are a symbol. The things you do are symbolic acts. This needs to be understood. Always consider the symbolic and ritualistic values of the actions you take and things you say. What do your words imply? What level of meaning do they have? Once you begin to think this way, you can plan your behavior so that it carries deep meaning and creates inspiration, pointing the way for the team . . . . An indication of success is your sense of integrity, which relates to the fitness and soundness of you as a person . . . . Be a role model of the degree of organization, discipline, follow-through and perseverance you ask from your people.

David Armistead

EACH ONE OF US needs to be a co-designer of our present. You need to be a co-designer of your future. What is a co-designer? A co-designer is one who takes responsibility for his or her being and shares that responsibility with the Creator and sponsors.

The Creator provided you with resources and talents, as well as inherent limitations. The resources are there. You need to use them.

Each person has many sponsors. Your primary sponsors are your family and friends.

Secondary sponsors may include institutions such as your place of employment, your place of worship and social organizations. These secondary sponsors are sometimes called *stakeholders* because we have a mutual interdependence in each others' successes. We all need to play out our parts as if we were members of a symphony orchestra.

Recently I had a physical fitness assessment. I met with a staff member at the fitness center to review the results and develop a plan to improve my overall health. Clayton, the staff member, explained to me that my physical fitness evaluation and program development were based on a composite baseline of age and weight. He suggested that we focus on the areas of what he called opportunities.

I needed some cardiovascular conditioning. Clayton helped me develop goals based on frequency, intensity and time of workouts.

(FIT!)   I shared some personal goals with Clayton, like my desire to lose ten pounds, and he helped me incorporate them in my program's goal.   I felt rather confident about the weight loss for I was used to giving up desserts, snacks and alcoholic beverages during Advent and Lent.   Clayton's comment was, "Why don't you start treating your body like a temple everyday?"   Moderation was the key!

In this illustration Clayton and I were co-designing where I wanted to be physically and positively affecting my thinking so that I might better achieve my goals.

This is just one dimension of your being.   Just think of all your spiritual and mental conditioning and that of friends and associates from which you draw support.   Many times you can combine your conditioning process, like riding a bike and listening to tapes at the same time.

George Sheehan, a cardiologist, author and runner, whom I followed for many years, wrote, "My fitness program was never a fitness program. It was a campaign, a revolution, a conversion.   I was determined to find myself.   And, in the process, found my body and the soul that went with it."

Today many business organizations expect individuals to self-manage their own careers which involves, among other things, keeping their job skills current while learning those skills required for the next step up.

This change in thinking is the result of a process commonly referred to in corporate North America as *business reengineering*.   It begins with rethinking the purposes of the business, and usually results in redesigning the core business and support processes beginning with customer requirements right through the supplier chain. Where successful, this has led to significant breakthroughs in productivity and customer service excellence.

Some of the fallout of this reengineering has changed the way large corporations relate to their employees. New patterns have emerged, sometimes referred to as paradigm shifts. There have been massive lay-offs at all levels of the corporation. The belief in long-term employment accompanied with a sense of job security and loyalty to the firm has been lost. This has driven fear and anxiety throughout the employee ranks of much of the corporate world.

Every day I see the negative impact this had and is having on the lives of employees and their families. Mostly employees in their forties or older are experiencing an adverse impact of this new employee contract. Younger employees have not had the same expectations ingrained in them and do not have the emotional and economic investments tied to the old system of thinking and behaving. Children in college, mortgages on their homes, unfulfilled expectations around retirement are just some of the pressures people are feeling. This, compounded by a flooded job market, and, in some cases, an inadequate set of technical skills, engenders a difficulty in being competitive and marketable in the current work force.

The organization usually provides the necessary training and development for one's future career opportunities. This is a new partnership arrangement and is a way of co-designing both the individual and the organization to be competitive, to be the best they can be! This is truly the way to foster and develop the new entrepreneurial spirit in the individual and the corporation.

Participative strategies are being used more and more by all organizations to foster commitment by their members at every level. These strategies are recognized as having a shared vision, purpose, values and common objectives which, it is believed, leads to a more effective and efficient organization with more satisfaction on the part of the participants.

From a philosophical point of view, we are all one with and in the universe. It is only possible to co-design with others. Then what do you do when someone does not want to co-design with you, like a spouse, a child, an employer or significant other? If the other does not cooperate, the design will be faulty.

You must find an alternative. Assuming that the relationship is important to you, that you value moving towards a state of interdependence and harmony, you must make yourself both inner-focused and outer-focused. Inwardly you must be centered which allows you to seek self-understanding. Ask yourself, "What is it that I desire? Why? How does that fit with my values and beliefs?"

The second step is to seek to understand the other person before asking that they understand you. This is done by dialoguing with the other person, and by active listening in an empathetic mode. You can be non-judgmental and caring while sharing the desire for collaboration and possibly identifying those behaviors together.

Tom was disgruntled with his career progress, and what his future would look like if he continued as he had been going. He had been searching for other alternatives for some time. His wife, Mary, was supportive of Tom's looking to improve their future.

Tom found an alternative in a completely different field, one that he could work on part-time and eventually build into a full-time business. Tom was excited and anxious to pursue this new line of work. He could see the possibilities for success and an improvement in their lifestyle.

When he shared with Mary what was involved, and her support role in the business, she was reluctant, to say the least. Tom first became upset, accusing Mary of being closed-minded and not giving the opportunity a chance. Mary's response? "We've had enough disruption in our lives. I don't need any more right now!!"

Now what do they do?

Try to identify those behaviors on both your parts that hinder an effective dialogue. This will take time if the initial resistance is strong and deeply-seeded, but it is possible to succeed. It is also possible to seek another alternative, such as acting independently. All actions have their consequences, few are life threatening, though all will affect the quality of your life. Be anchored in your vision, purpose and beliefs!

How will you be the architect of your own future? Think of yourself as a sculptor molding your being with clay rather than stone. Clay allows you to be adaptive and flexible. How will you positively or negatively impact others' lives by being their co-designer? What can you do in your role as co-designer to assure that you will enhance others in their lives?

PRINCIPLE V:
I CELEBRATE THE PRESENT
AND GIVE THANKS

Most people are about as happy as they make up their minds to be.

Abraham Lincoln

The greatest discovery of my age is that [people] can change their circumstances by changing the attitude of their minds.

William James

THE PRESENT IS THE GIFT OF LIFE!

The present is our link to the future and to our memories of the past. The present is the only place that really exists. It is the only place where we can be truly alive in our humanity; the breath of life is the present. We can celebrate our life here and now.

You can accept the here and now, what you have been given in capabilities and what potentialities you have yet to experience. Choose an attitude of prosperity. Seek out whatever you need to prosper and grow. What would this mean to you? For each person, it would be different.

A personal breakthrough I experienced was understanding what wealth creation meant to me and for me. I used to narrowly think of it in terms of monetary assets and value. This restricted me in seeking wealth and feeling comfortable valuing it. Today, wealth has a much broader meaning to me. *Any asset which brings good to others and to myself without harm or deprivation to any is wealth.*

I associate the creation of wealth with the responsibility of stewardship. To manage wealth for the welfare of all, to treat it as a gift rather than a possession for my own use, is responsible stewardship. This new consciousness is freeing, empowering and challenging! I want to create as much wealth in as many forms as I possibly can. The personal challenge is twofold — creation and stewardship.

You can look at this principle, to celebrate the present and give thanks, in light of the other four principles. As you practice the first four principles, the fifth principle takes on greater meaning. As you gain self-knowledge, develop and understand your core values and beliefs, you have a context to better understand the purpose of the present in your life. Based on this broader meaning, you take responsibility for your thoughts and actions which will be guided by your own design.

> Celebration and giving thanks has been another attitude shift for me. My conditioning had been to focus on what was yet to do, to improve, perfect, to focus on the void, rather than to be thankful for what was accomplished. I did not celebrate the achievement, the here and now! I did not know how to be truly alive. We all need to value and appreciate ourselves, and each other, individually and in community.

You can learn to value and appreciate yourself! You can transcend your limited sense of being and connect with all of nature of which you are only a small part. No matter how grand or how painful your existence may be for the moment, in the greater scheme of things in the universe, it is but a finite moment, a speck of time.

One afternoon while walking and meditating the following prayer song came into my mind, first in melody and then, as the music flowed, so did the words:

> *Thank you, Lord, for giving me this day!*
> *Thank you, Lord, for showing me the way!*
> *Thank you, Lord, for being with me today;*
> *Thank you, Lord, for loving me each day.*
> *Thank you, Lord, for blessing me this way!*

Thank you, Lord!!
Thank you, Lord!!
Alleluia, Alleluia!!

I try to discipline myself each day so that I may put my life in perspective by focusing on nature, the mountains, the sky, the animals and all living things, and to offer thanks to the Creator for the beauty I have before me.

These five principles put into daily practice will help you truly be alive in the moment. You will have regard for yourself, for others and for the world unfolding about you.

Think of these five principles as a rope made of five individual strands. Each strand consists of many strong fibers. These strands woven together make a strong and durable rope that will be your lifeline to success, fulfillment and happiness!

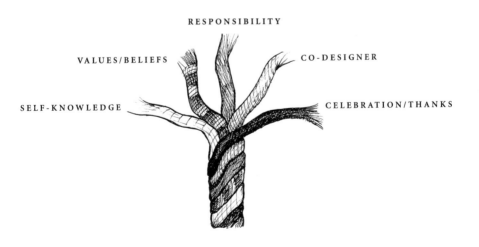

RESPONSIBILITY

VALUES/BELIEFS   CO-DESIGNER

SELF-KNOWLEDGE   CELEBRATION/THANKS

In Part II of this text, you will be provided with conceptual tools and mental techniques that will guide you on this wonderful journey called living!

In the next chapter, I will share with you some of the obstacles that we all experience that sometimes prevent us from engaging life positively and interfere with fulfilling our potential.

OVERCOMING LIFE'S HINDRANCES AND OBSTACLES

God, grant me the serenity
to accept the things
I cannot change,
Courage to change
the things I can,
And the wisdom
to know the difference.

Rheinhold Niebuhr

LIFE IS A PROCESS. The very nature of our existence from birth to death is motion. As we mature from dependence to independence to interdependence, we see change as our one constant, change to the world and change to our own spirit. This transcendence of the human spirit is described over and over again in the great writings of the mystics and prophets.

We also know from our life experience that our existence here on earth is not perfect or pure in nature. Life is, of itself, a constant struggle for survival and growth. Both within ourselves and within the world, we experience good and evil forces. We constantly have to make choices about what to do and what not to do.

These choices can be conscious ones or unconscious ones. If they are unconscious choices, they are usually labeled as habits. Habits are behavioral responses that have become conditioned by spaced repetition and positive reinforcement over time. We have a gut feeling that something is right or wrong, good or bad. It is intuitive. Most of our routine behaviors fall into this category; things we do without even thinking. Biases and stereotyping are examples of the mindsets that support these behaviors.

Overcoming the Horrendous Years

Let me share with you some of my struggles so that you know that I am not all theory. I call this particular story The Horrendous Years. It occurred seven years ago. We could not have survived them as well as we did without faith, family and friends.

In retrospect our children tell us that they learned so much during that period, they had so many wonderful family experiences, and they would not like to think that it could have been different. The results were beneficial. We experienced much joy and pain throughout this period in time. Most importantly, our relationships with each other grew immeasurably in richness and depth.

We lived in Toronto, Canada. I had a well-paying position with a national oil company, albeit I was beginning to become bored. Our home was owned free and clear! We had a close group of friends, actually six families, that were our extended family.

It seemed to me to be time to make a move. My wife, Pat, is innately cautious. She looked at a possible move with skepticism and alarm. "Why make the change? Everything is wonderful in our lives right now. You may want to be closer to your family, but I do not get along with them. They've never really cared for me."

I could see opportunity calling. We would move to the States. Our children would experience a new setting and be able to exercise their dual citizenship, United States and Canadian. We would live near my aging parents. I would go into business with my brother. My career would be exciting, challenging and a true opportunity to put into practice my theories on how to run a business effectively. We would have a larger home, live near the water, live closer to nature.

We did it. We moved to Scarborough, Maine: I, with great hopes for our future; Pat, with some trepidation and lots of love and support. We were all committed to making this work!

I will spare you the anguish and the details, but share instead some causative factors and results from this intensive learning experience. Briefly, after being in the family business for about a year, I began to realize how well I knew myself (Principle I), and the significance of the value and belief differences (Principle II) between my brother and myself.

In deciding to enter the business, I was so blinded by the hope of material gain that I down-played how different my brother and I were as people. These differences included how to build a business, particularly regarding staffing, the management of people, and how to establish the kind of work climate that allowed all people to perform well. There were basic differences in how we believed one should work with customers and suppliers.

I soon recognized that I could not sufficiently influence my brother's thinking, nor could I accept his behavior as demonstrated in his use of power over me and the others who worked *for him,* not *with us.* These conflicts took a personal toll on our relationship which led me to realize that I must leave the business. My brother agreed. Unfortunately, we could not agree on the method to end the business relationship even though we had an up-front separation agreement should such a separation occur.

After twenty-six months I did leave the business. In retrospect, I asked myself, "Bob, if you hired yourself as a consultant to advise on whether or not to join your brother's firm, what advice would you have given to yourself?" I knew then that I had overlooked the importance of shared values to a relationship of any kind, and especially a business relationship.

We sometimes do not realize when we are suffering how much it hurts those who love us. At this time, Pat sent me a card to express her caring and support, as well as her pain and anguish.

Everyone is afraid of change . . . I hope it
helps to know I believe in you.

Her note said, "I know the past couple of weeks have
been difficult. My heart goes out to you. I am having the
most difficult time dealing with how your family treats us. It
is incomprehensible to me. It feels like someone has torn me
apart every time."

Many other things occurred during that same period
and in the following two years.

My eldest daughter went away to school only to come
home unwell. She was diagnosed with Obsessive Compulsive
Disorder.

My aged parents both died. Dad died in the hospital
of heart failure after nine months of near recovery from a seri-
ous car accident. Mother died about one year later with
Alzheimer's. Handling family matters and business matters
was very stressful for all the members of my immediate family.

I attempted to start up a new business venture six
months after leaving the family business only to face a down-
turn in the economy, most particularly in the marketplace I
was trying to enter.

I had three major surgeries in less than twelve
months: a torn rotator cuff repair on the left shoulder from a
fall on the ice during business travel, and a double hip
replacement after a long debilitating arthritic condition.
At the same time as the surgeries, I started my consulting
practice which required extensive travel.

My wife was diagnosed with a chronic muscle tissue
disorder. We had exhausted our savings and assumed significant debt trying both to maintain our lifestyle and put our
second daughter through university.

This was an exceedingly trying time for Pat and me. Fortunately, we had tremendous support from family members and close friends. Our household was never empty, especially during the holidays! Pat and I also had our faith and were very active in our local parish. Our prayer life was strong. The weight of these burdens was not as immobilizing as I would have imagined, which I attribute to our faith and the love we received from our family and friends.

As my consulting practice began to grow, I spent much of my time in the Toronto area, a long-standing network of ours. I approached a Canadian company that was looking for an internal consultant, assuming that they might want to subcontract some of their work. After exploring the potential opportunity of the internal consulting position, I accepted that challenge.

For nine months I commuted between Maine and Toronto before relocating my family, only to have us need to relocate to the southwestern part of the United States seven months later. This became a time of healing, of nurture and growth.

If you had asked us to project two years ago where we would be today and what roads we would have travelled, we could not have done so. Life is a continuous surprise to us! All we know is that it is getting better. The secret seems to be in the process and flow of one's life rather than in the tangible, material results one acquires along the way. Our greatest gifts in life have been our relationships with our children, our family, our friends and our God!

During this time, Kymberly, my eldest daughter, gave me a beautiful card with a verse by Dorothy R. Colgan.

Thank you for believing in me when I found
it difficult to believe in myself . . . for saying

what I've needed to hear sometimes, instead of what I wanted to hear . . . for siding with me . . . and for giving me another side to consider.

Thank you for keeping me from taking myself, or my problems, too seriously . . . and for not laughing at me when I was too sensitive to laugh at myself.

Thank you for opening yourself up to me . . . and for trusting me with your thoughts and disappointments and dreams . . . for knowing you can depend on me, for asking my help when you needed it.

Thank you for putting so much thought and care and imagination into our relationship . . . for sharing so many nice times . . . and making so many special memories with me.

Thank you for always being honest with me . . . being kind to me . . . being there for me.

Thank you for being a friend to me in so many truly meaningful ways.

Lessons Learned

All of us have experienced or heard similar stories about overcoming adversity in one's life. It is what one learns from these experiences and the sharing of others' experiences that help us fashion the way we live. Think and reflect for yourself. Ask yourself, "What should I keep on doing, stop doing, start doing to prepare myself for the adversities as I confront my life journey?"

When I reflect on what I learned from these trials, several lessons surface:

In Relationship: Building and sustaining relationships through love is critical to our well-being. By incorporating common purpose, shared values, perceived trust and equitable use of power, relationships can grow in trust, respect and mutual regard.

When I speak about "in relationship," I am referring to relationship in three realms. The first realm is living in relationship with yourself. This is the love of self. It is through loving oneself that you learn to love others. You respect yourself, care for yourself and value your own existence and the contribution you make to others.

The second realm is in relationship to others. It means truly to care about and respect others. It is to value the existence of others, and to understand and respect their needs as you honor your own. Referring to our definition of self-management, it recognizes the interdependence between all of us and the potential for synergy.

The third realm is to be in relationship with our spirit. In our model of the whole person, we recognize the relationship between mind, body and spirit. It is the spirit which elevates us to a higher level of being.

In corporate America today, we are yearning for these kinds of relationships. We need to come back into balance. When I say we, I am referring to all employees and all key stakeholders in the corporate structure. It is not them or us, it is we who have to re-define and re-design the integrity of the corporate structure.

Common Purpose: My brother and I entered into an employment contract without a shared vision and mission which eventually undermined the desired monetary goal. Within a relationship of this kind, there needs to be a common shared purpose. The common bond between my brother and me was fraternal. It was birth given. It was not a true love relationship. Within our homes, within our communities and within our corporations, we need to be able to strive for a common purpose and a shared vision of how to make that purpose be alive!

Shared Values: My brother and I do not share a common set of values on business ethics, partnership, employee, customer and supplier relations or on the necessary requirements to build a business. This was my biggest mistake!

These three elements, in relationship, common purpose and shared values, are like strands of a rope. The wholeness and strength of the rope is dependent on how these strands are woven together. If the value structures are not compatible, the relationship will wither and a common purpose will not be achieved. Individuals are attracted to and repelled by one's underlying values and their compatibility with these values. This is why we see today a common practice in many corporations of articulating their values and demonstrating the associated behavioral attributes.

Use of Power: The politics of a situation are critical to bringing about change. How are economic decisions made? What are the economics of the situation or relationship? What is being exchanged between the parties in the relationship? Who has the balance of power? Who speaks to whom about what? Who can influence whom about what? Are there alliances? These are just some of the questions to ponder before entering an important relationship.

Family of Origin and Family of Choice: We have no choice about our family of origin but, as we mature, we can become more selective in relationships through common interests and values. Sometimes we grow closer to or draw away from natural family members. Many times we form close bonds with friends who become as family. Scripture illustrates both a need to separate, at times, from your family of origin because of differing beliefs, and, at times, a returning to your family of origin as in the story of The Prodigal Son. When you have invested in developing mutually caring and loving relationships, in a time of need, family and friends come in a giving way to support you.

Faith in a Loving God: This belief, coupled with communication with God, is a strong power to allow you to overcome adversity. There is a given strength in saying and believing the words, "God, I do not know what to do; I leave it in Your hands." God's love enables me to smile at the world with all its miracles, and to smile at others in such a way that the world seems to smile back at me. This positive energy radiates out of me to others and brings back positive responses.

These are just some of the lessons I learned. All of the lessons I learned are supported by the five principles, the methods and techniques contained in these writings. They hold true as a guide and discipline to living a fuller life both inside and outside the corporation. They truly will ignite and sustain a new entrepreneurial spirit. If nothing else, I am dedicated to a lifelong learning and conditioning process for myself. The personal challenge is in the action, the doing, the daily discipline of practice!

The application of principles, methods, and techniques are described in Part II of this text entitled, Striving for Results: A Guide to Creating Your Success.

for quick reference . . .

THE FIVE BASIC PRINCIPLES

I know myself.

I establish a personal set of values and beliefs.

I take responsibility for who and what I am.

I am a co-designer of my life, who I am, and who I want to become.

I celebrate the present, and give thanks!

Are you ready to start?

Striving For Results:
A Guide to Creating Your Success

INTRODUCTION

*We hold these Truths to be self-evident, that
all Men (and Women) are created equal, that
they are endowed by their Creator with certain unalienable Rights, that among these
are Life, Liberty, and the Pursuit of
Happiness . . . .*

Declaration of Independence, 1776

*One's philosophy is not best expressed in
words; it's expressed in the choices one
makes. In the long run, we shape our lives
and we shape ourselves. The process never
ends until we die. And the choices we make
are ultimately our responsibility.*

Eleanor Roosevelt

TODAY'S CHALLENGE for all of us is to believe that we can control our own destiny; that we can have a sense of balance in our lives. Like managing any of our affairs, we need frameworks to help us think about what we want to manage, and some tools and techniques to get the tasks done. All this is provided for you in this section. More importantly, the essential ingredient for your success is YOU — your will and your desire!

This section will help you to focus on both the results you determine are important to be successful in your life and the process that will help you map out your journey.

Helpful Hints

You have many choices on how to use this section:

• Work on it both individually and in teams with your family members, or fellow workers.

• Develop a schedule for yourself, share it with others for support and to reinforce your commitment.

• Link this set of activities to other work you are doing to create synergy, e.g. Performance Management; Career Development; Strategic Planning; schedules and other planning activities or personal development programs.

• Most of all, HAVE FUN! Celebrate your accomplishments as you progress through this section.

INSPIRATION AT WORK

OVERVIEW

All things are created twice: first, mentally, and second, physically. Begin with the end in mind.

Stephen R. Covey

All our dreams can come true — if we have the courage to pursue them.

Walt Disney

I challenge you to make your life a master-piece. I challenge you to join the ranks of those people who live what they teach, who walk their talk.

Anthony Robbins

THIS GUIDE TO CREATING YOUR SUCCESS
consists of the following four chapters:

-A Way to Achieve Your Goals

-An Approach to Self-Management

-A Self-Motivation Process

-A Way to Influence Others to Help You Succeed

In this overview, I will give a brief outline of each of these subject areas. But first let me spend a few moments expressing my thoughts on the reason for this series and how you can use it productively. It is all in the title "Striving for Results." The *striving* is what you're doing and the *results* are why you're doing it. All those hours at the plant or office, all the assignments, all the projects, all the changes in priorities, hours and hours of activities.

- Why are you doing this?

- What are you trying to achieve?

- What returns are you getting on your investment?

- What's in it for you?

- What sense of satisfaction do you derive from what you are doing?

You have your own answers to these questions. Part II will help you to discover these answers and to evaluate whether or not you want to make any changes.

Most, if not all, of what we do is (or was) purposeful activity! To the extent that we can bring these purposes to our conscious awareness and crystallize our thinking in terms of goals or results that we want to achieve, we can be more effective in carrying out the many activities on a moment-to-moment, day-to-day basis that lead us to achieving these results. We can then manage our time more effectively as well as having a greater understanding and appreciation of what we are doing and why. We can begin to share this with others and seek their support. We can contribute to one another's success.

You see it is all in the title **Striving for Results.** This is sure to give you food for thought as well as some practical tools that can get you started in applying some of these ideas.

CAPABILITY DEVELOPMENT

```
STRATEGIC MANAGEMENT
  • Vision/Mission
  • Values/Beliefs
  • Key Result Areas

BUILDING RELATIONSHIPS
  • Stakeholder Identification
  • Influencing Skills

SELF-MANAGEMENT
  • Goal Achievement
  • Personal Discipline
  • Tools/Techniques

SELF-MOTIVATION
  • Positive Mental
    Conditioning
  • Tools/Techniques
```

AS YOU FOCUS ON STRIVING FOR RESULTS, you will naturally improve your performance capabilities. The chapters in this section are designed to create exponential growth.

In **A Way To Achieve Your Goals,** you will investigate your personal strategic management framework, including a personal vision/mission, set of personal values, and key result areas.

In **An Approach to Self-Management,** you will learn to value the philosophy of self-management, obtain tools and techniques to implement the process, and learn how to enhance your process continually to achieve both short- and long-term goals.

In **A Self-Motivation Process,** you will begin to understand goal-setting as a powerful motivating force. You will easily overcome obstacles to your own inner motivation, and develop positive mental conditioning techniques which reinforce your desire to succeed.

In **A Way To Influence Others to Help You Succeed,** you will learn to appreciate interpersonal relationship skills and how they impact your success. You will also learn what these skills require and how to identify key stakeholders to build mutually beneficial relationships.

Personal Development Exercise #1

T H O U G H T   S T A R T E R S

A S   A   S E T - U P   for the next step entitled "A Way to Achieve Your Goals," get a notebook and entitle it **Striving for Results.** This will become your workbook — a journal for your development. On the first page, write "Thought Starters."

- Why are you doing what you are doing:
    - all those hours at home, school, factory or office?
    - all the assignments and projects?
    - all the changes in priorities?

- What are you trying to achieve?

- What do you want in return?

Now, referring to the questions that I cited above, divide the page into two columns:

1. *Why* I am in my current job/career/vocation

2. *What* I do

Then begin to make lists. Brainstorm under each of those columns. That is, *why* are you in your job — the many reasons; and *what activities* are you engaged in either relating to or through your job. Try to fill one or two pages. This exercise will prove valuable to you as we proceed.

A WAY TO ACHIEVE YOUR GOALS

Where there is no vision, the people perish.

Proverbs 29:18

If one advances confidently in the direction of his dreams, and endeavors to live the life which he has imagined, he will meet with a success unexpected in common hours.

Henry David Thoreau
Walden

I WANT YOU TO UNDERSTAND what
goals are and how they enable you to achieve the results you
want. I will explain some of the common characteristics that
we all share as human beings in the process of goal-setting. I
will identify some of the benefits that you are likely to derive
from setting goals.

An important part of goal-setting is knowing how to
get started. This guide will provide you with a framework for
goal-setting. Once you understand this framework and begin
to apply it through the personal development exercises, you
will be taking the first important steps in the self-management
of your personal life and career.

What are Goals?

Goals are simply the desired results you want to
achieve over time. What are some of the common characteristics that we, as human beings, share regarding the process of
goal-setting? First, why do I use the phrase "process of goal-
setting?" As a process, I mean that goal-setting is ongoing,
dynamic, ever-changing, and evolving. There is nothing
static about people setting goals.

Reflect on your own past for a moment. Haven't
your career goals changed over time? Maybe not the long-
term goal, but I'll bet that what you need to achieve along the
way has become clearer to you. Got the idea? We change,
and our situations and our environments change over time.
We develop new interests, discover new abilities; our manager may change, or a new position may require a move to
another location.

Sometimes we may feel the emergence of conflicting or competing goals, either consciously or unconsciously. This may create a state of ambivalence or "mixed feelings" inside us. These goals may be divergent (leading in different directions) or convergent (leading in a similar direction). They may be sequential; that is, one before the other in timing.

It is important for us to develop an appreciation and understanding of these characteristics of the goal-setting process. We need ways to handle these characteristics effectively, so we can have a sense of accomplishment and joy in working towards, and actually attaining, the results we want.

You may be asking yourself: "Why are goals so important anyway?" or "What benefits could I derive by developing a clear set of goals for myself?" Here is a simple list of benefits for you to consider:

GOALS:

-help you to CONCENTRATE

-add to your SELF-RESPECT

-create a SENSE OF PURPOSE and

      ANTICIPATION IN LIFE

-can help you to MAKE GOOD DECISIONS

-help you to SAVE TIME

-are great CONFIDENCE BUILDERS

-can REDUCE CONFLICT

Getting Started:
A Framework for Goal-Setting

BEFORE DEVELOPING A SET OF GOALS that will direct and guide you towards achieving your desired results, there are four simple and creative steps I suggest that you follow. These steps will provide you with a framework for goal-setting.

The first step is to write a **Mission Statement.** That's what I said — Mission Statement! Think of James Bond or Luke Skywalker in *Star Wars* in terms of a mission. When you use the expression, "He or she has a mission in life," what does it mean? It usually means that such a person has dedicated himself or herself to accomplishing a specific task. Can you think of your current job in terms of a mission? Think about it. Why are you dedicating your time and energies to your job?

The second step is to create a **Vision** of yourself having achieved your Mission in your current job or career. Who would you be? What would you be like? Where would you be? Who would be with you? Close your eyes and put your imagination to work.

This is the **Power of Visualization,** your imagination put to work! The more you can visualize who and what you want to be, the greater your chances are of achieving what you want. In psychological terms, this is referred to as "a self-fulfilling prophecy." Think of what you do to yourself every day with either positive or negative thoughts you have about yourself — "I can do it," "I know I can't," or "I'm afraid I'm going to fail," "I'm not good enough" — these are powerful thoughts that will either help or hinder you in achieving what you want to achieve. This is as true in the short term, that is, the day-to-day accomplishments, as it is for the long term, that is, what you want to be or have in the future.

The third step is **Basic Beliefs/Values.** In a recent talk I gave, I mentioned the importance of each and every one of us becoming aware and conscious of our personal values to guide our behavior and our goal choices. Someone asked, "Do you mean our religious beliefs or something like that?" This person was close in her association. You see, our beliefs, or what we learn to value in life, are very much influenced by relationships of authority in our lives such as those with parents, church, school and the laws of our community. Remember as you were growing up, you would hear "Don't do that;" "No, don't touch;" or "That was really nice of you; I'm so proud of you!" You heard what was "good" and what was "bad;" what was preferred or desired behavior and what was not.

As we mature as individuals and want to exercise more and more responsibility for managing our own lives, we have to establish our own set of values to guide our behavior and choices. I mentioned earlier that our goals may be in conflict with one another; so may our values. When these conflicts arise, they are usually associated with feelings of frustration, tension, nervousness, and sometimes even guilt — for example, "I know I should do this rather than that and I'll probably feel badly and sorry if I don't do what I should."

To the extent that we can clarify our own values or beliefs (that is, what they are and how they are related to one another), we can make better decisions on how to manage conflicting goals and values. Later, in the personal development exercise portion of this chapter, you will have an opportunity to begin to identify your own personal and professional values.

The fourth and final step in developing this framework is to identify the **Key Result Areas (KRAs)** that will contribute significantly to your successfully achieving your

Mission and fulfilling your Vision. What key areas are the critical few that you need to work? For example, Physical and Mental Conditioning, Job Skills, Team Relationships, Family, Job Performance, Finance, and Spirituality. Think of your total development as a person who has dedicated yourself to achieve a specific task (Mission). What or whom will your success be dependent upon? Make sure you have identified a Key Result Area that will cover each of these. These KRAs will help you to develop your specific goals and to better focus your energies.

The following chart gives an illustration of the wholeness and potential of a person. Each element converges in the center and makes up part of the whole person. As you set your goals, keep this in mind to help you keep a balance in your goal-setting and, ultimately, in your life.

THE   WHOLE   PERSON   "WHEEL"
PERSONAL   POTENTIALS

Here is another visual portrayal of the wholeness of the individual and the relationship of wholeness to one's well-being. It is so easy for us to lose perspective and to focus overly on one area of our development to the exclusion of others. Prolonged periods of time doing this will drive us into personal turmoil or even crisis. Reflect on your personal experience to date. Has this happened to you?

THE WHOLE PERSON

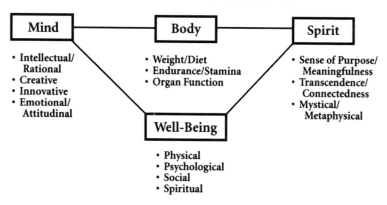

Now, let us look at a definition of **Health** before beginning our practice session. This definition, like that of goal-setting, is process-oriented, that is, health, too, is not static but on-going.

WHAT IS HEALTH?

**HEALTH IS A SYNERGISTIC OR COOPERATIVE
PROCESS WHEREBY:**
All human experience is enhanced –
the body, the mind, and the spirit
Every way that you meet
your environment,
all your physical, intellectual,
and psychological actions,
inter-actions, and reactions,
is increasingly positive.

**HEALTH IS NOT STATIC. IT IS AN ONGOING
CONDITION OF CONSTANT IMPROVEMENT.**

OUR HEALTH IS HOLISTIC! It is more
than just our physical health or mental health or spiritual
health. It is all of these and their relatedness to each other.
Don't neglect one for the other. To excel at any one over time,
we need to work on all of our health. That is what creates
well-being!

One of the easiest ways to maintain this delicate
balance called health is by being aware of your goals. Let's
set up the framework now in Exercise #2.

Personal Development Exercise #2:

D E V E L O P I N G   Y O U R   O W N   G O A L - S E T T I N G   F R A M E W O R K

Now that you know the three steps to developing your Goal-Setting Framework, let us draw on the exercise you did in the "Overview" and apply the ideas you generated to the following exercises.

Drafting a Mission Statement

T U R N   T O   Y O U R   W O R K B O O K and glance through your Thought Starters list. Leave some blank sheets (six to eight) and then entitle one "Draft Mission Statement." You will continue to add to your Thought Starters list at least weekly.

In about three to five lines, describe what your mission will have accomplished at its completion (possibly two to five years from now). It should answer in *Results* terms why you are doing what you are doing. It should describe what you will be like, where you will be, and what you will have accomplished (quantitatively and qualitatively).

Have a go at it!

Creating a "Vision" of Yourself and Your Situation

BE CREATIVE IN CREATING YOUR VISION. Use your imagination; daydream! Develop your vision over time. First, start with writing a short story about yourself in your workbook entitled "Creating A Vision of Myself." Begin by thinking of the questions I raised earlier:

- Who would you be?
- What would you be like?
- Where would you be?
- Who would be with you?

Or . . .

Create a collage on a poster board with pictures out of a magazine or printed words or symbols depicting your vision. Think of other imaginative ways of visualizing the accomplishments of your mission. Share these ideas with others, for example, your spouse, close friends, and your manager.

Basic Beliefs/Values Statement

LET'S OPEN OUR WORKBOOKS to a blank sheet and entitle it "Basic Beliefs/Values Statement Exercise." We can categorize values into three groupings: performance values, social/inter-personal values, and spiritual values. If there are other categories you would like to use instead, feel free to do so.

Let me take a moment to elaborate on each one of these value groupings. **Performance values** can refer to our achievement orientation, our attitude or orientation towards work such as the production of things, and the style in which we work, such as our aggressiveness, compulsivity or tendency towards perfection. **Social/interpersonal values** can be illustrated by such terms as trust, honesty, openness, mutual respect, and fairness. **Spiritual values** are usually associated with the part of human existence that goes beyond those things we can readily observe or measure, such as our belief in the meaning or purpose of our lives; the supernatural.

For each of the above groupings of values, make a column on this sheet of paper for a brainstorming exercise. Now generate as many ideas and thoughts that you can under each of these groupings. Don't restrict yourself.

On the next sheet of paper, write the title "My Basic Beliefs and Values." Either in point form or in brief paragraphs, possibly under each grouping, pull your thoughts and ideas together and formulate what you now consider to be your beliefs and values. Don't forget that this is a first draft; therefore, you will most likely want to revise it later as you have more time to think about it.

Key Result Areas: "The Critical Few"

T H E R E   A R E   M A N Y   T H I N G S or areas you can work on that can help you achieve your mission. However, if you were asked to identify the "critical few" areas (three to six) that would be essential to the accomplishment of your Mission, what would they be? Remember the examples I used earlier: Physical and Mental Conditioning, Job Skills, Team Relationships, Family, Job Performance, etc. Now list your own KRAs.

Test each item in this list against these questions:

1.   Is it essential to achieving my mission?

2.   Do I spend time considering ways to improve performance in this area? (Or should I be?)

3.   If this area were eliminated, in what way would my mission be affected?

4.   Is this an area that should receive constant and careful attention?

Now you have your "Framework for Goal-Setting," for getting started. With this cornerstone in place, you will have a sound foundation for developing meaningful goals and managing your way to success — means to self-management.

AN APPROACH TO SELF-MANAGEMENT

It is the mind that maketh good or ill, that maketh wretch or happy, rich or poor.

Edmund Spenser

Our doubts are traitors, and make us lose the good we oft might win, by fearing to attempt.

William Shakespeare

YOU HAVE ALREADY MADE A BEGINNING
toward self-management by formulating your Framework for
Goal-Setting. As we move along through this personal development program, continually go back over what you have
done for two reasons:

(1) As a reference and building block to what you
are currently working on;

(2) To modify what you have already done based
on new ideas and experiences.

Remember, the process of goal-setting is dynamic,
ongoing, and evolving by its very nature.

In this chapter we'll focus our attention on the topic
of self-management. I'll explain what I mean by "self-
management" and I'll outline a management process to assist
you in applying the concept of self-management.

What is Self-Management?

T O   M A N A G E is defined as: "To control the movement or behavior of; to have charge of; direct; to succeed in
accomplishing." (*Webster's New World Dictionary,* William
Collins Publishers, Incorporated, 1979.)

Let's take this definition and add the word *self* to it.
Self-management means:

a. To be in control of your own behavior; movement, or
resourcefulness.

b.   To be self-directed, coming from within.

c.   To be neither totally independent nor dependent, but rather a striving for interdependence, a harmony with others and the world of which you are a part.

d.   To accomplish progressively pre-determined and emerging, worthwhile, realistic, and meaningful goals.

Right now, let's focus our attention on managing for RESULTS (Remember our theme is "Striving for Results."). Before we move on, let me summarize by presenting this brief outline of our goal-setting framework:

GOAL-SETTING FRAMEWORK

MY MISSION • Why I am dedicated to _____.	
MY VISION • Where and what I would be, having achieved my mission	
MY BASIC BELIEFS/VALUES • What is important to me • What is good for me	MY KEY RESULT AREAS • It is essential • Improved performance desired • Constant/careful attention

Self-Management Process

THE SELF-MANAGEMENT PROCESS enables you to get where you want to go, to achieve the Mission you have set for yourself, to realize the Vision you are creating. This Self-Management Process consists of four basic components, and each component has a number of elements as indicated in the following diagram:

SELF-MANAGEMENT PROCESS

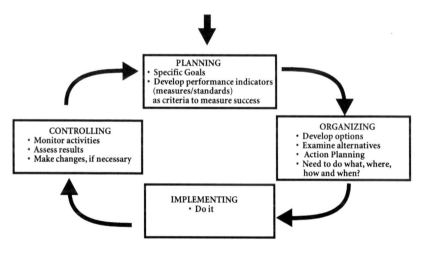

97

I will elaborate on each of these components of the process and give some illustrations.

Planning — Using a time frame of three months to one year:

-Develop a set of specific goals under each Key Result Area. These are short-term, realistic results that you need to obtain to move you towards your long-term mission.

-Develop performance indicators for each goal that you set. These are measures or standards that will enable you to know what progress you are making. For example, performance indicators can be project completion times, improving job skills/techniques to a specific standard, a certain amount or level of competence training, etc.

Organizing — You only have a certain amount of time and energy to expend. Also, there is usually more than one way to achieve your desired results — one may be more efficient and effective than another.

-Given the above, develop as many options as possible to achieve your goals; examine each alternative and select the best.

-Action Plan — now you're ready to list your goals, what you need to do (activities), including how, where, and when.

Implementing — This is simply putting into action what you have written in your Action Plan.

Controlling — This is an ongoing activity. It involves reviewing your plans regularly to assure you are on course in attaining the results you desire. At times you may have to change the way you are going about achieving your goals, and at other times you may want to alter your goals.

A Needed Discipline

BEFORE I GO ANY FURTHER, let me say a few words about what it takes to apply this whole approach to STRIVING FOR RESULTS. If you have not already realized it, it is not easy! I never said it would be, did I? It takes a great deal of SELF- DISCIPLINE. The degree to which you put time aside to do the necessary work is up to you, and your RESULTS will probably relate in direct proportion to the energy and effort you put into it.

However, I will give you some suggestions regarding how to organize and apply your time:

(1)   Take full advantage of this guide to Creating Your Success and do all the exercises, realizing it's hard the first time around because a lot of what you are being asked to do is new to you.

(2)   Each twelve-month cycle, follow this schedule or a similar one.

• At the start of the 4th quarter, do the exercises in the first three chapters of Part II.

• At the end of the 1st quarter, review and update your Goal-Setting Framework and your Self-Management Process.

• At the end of the 4th quarter, review your results and make whatever changes are required.

(3)   Share your framework and goals with others who can contribute to your success, e.g. manager, work unit members, spouse and others.

Professional Development Exercise #3:

DEVELOPING YOUR OWN SELF-MANAGEMENT PROCESS

This practice session will get you started on a Self-Management Process.

Self-Management Process Exercise

A. Referring to your Goal-Setting Framework, take a blank sheet of paper for each Key Result Area that you have developed and entitle it "Key Result Area Worksheet." In the upper left-hand corner, write out a Key Result Area on each sheet. Divide the sheet in half to create two columns. At the top of one column, write "Specific Goals," and at the top of the other column, write "Performance Indicators." Now write down as many specific goals relating to that Key Result Area and its respective performance indicators as you can.

B. After generating a number of goals and their performance indicators under each Key Result Area, rank the specific goals under each Key Result Area in order of priority using criteria such as: attainable, measurable, worthwhile, importance to mission.

C1. Take each goal that meets the criteria and develop options of how to carry that goal out, for example: what do I need to do, where, how, and when?

C2. Examine the alternatives.

D. Develop an action plan for each Key Result Area. Do this by taking a sheet of paper and for a title write in the Key Result Area. Now, divide that sheet of paper into four columns as illustrated below.

Goals	Activities (What, Where, How)	Timing	Progress Remarks

Fill in an action plan for each Key Result Area as suggested. Now you are ready to take action and monitor yourself along the way.

As I mentioned earlier, I never said it would be easy. However, given that you have come this far, look what you have accomplished. Look how much better you know yourself and where you want to go. Don't you now have a better idea of where you want to be and how you want to get there? Don't look at this as a finished product, but only as a beginning, as a journey towards self-discovery and being self-directed. Believe me, if you have come this far in following the process that I have outlined for you, you are already way ahead of many individuals who have not yet acquired the self-discipline or the tools to set goals.

In our next chapter, "A SELF-MOTIVATION PROCESS," you will see how what you have already done will significantly contribute to your motivation towards success in achieving your desired results. You will also better understand how motivation works and what you can do to be self-motivated.

A SELF-MOTIVATION PROCESS

When I am afraid, O Most High,
I put my trust in you.
I trust in God and praise his promise;
in him I trust, and I will not be afraid.
What can mere man do to me?

Psalms 56: 3-4

It's not what people do to us that hurts us. In the most fundamental sense it is our chosen response to what they do to us that hurts us.

Stephen R. Covey

YOU MUST HAVE GUESSED IT BY NOW
and, better yet, have experienced it. That's right, GOAL-
SETTING is a means of self-motivation. In this chapter, we
will build on what we have already learned. We will explore
the subject of motivation and how you can apply what you
have learned to help you to succeed in achieving your desired
results. There are also some other techniques that I will share
with you that you can use for self-motivation: self-talk,
positive affirmations, positive visualization, self-disclosure,
and mind mapping.

What is Motivation?

THE TERM MOTIVE applies to any internal force
that activates a person and gives direction to behavior. There
are a number of terms associated with different aspects of
motivation, such as needs, drives, instincts, incentives and
goals. There are also other factors that affect behavior like
interests, attitudes and purposes.

Motivation itself can be viewed in terms of three
major components. The first is energizing — a force that
arouses you to action. The second involves direction — you
direct your efforts to certain tasks or situations and not to
others. Finally, motivation involves perseverance — meaning
that you will maintain some tasks as compared to others that
may be over quite quickly.

Goal-Setting

GOAL-SETTING is actually a theory of motivation based on the assumption that people behave rationally and consciously. This does not rule out irrational or unconscious behavior. It just states that there is a relationship between conscious goals, intentions, and task performance. The basic premise is that conscious ideas regulate your actions. Goal attainment and intentions are what you are consciously trying to do, particularly as they relate to your future wants and desires.

As I implied before, goals have two major functions. They are a basis for motivation and they direct behavior. However, in order to positively influence your performance, you must first be aware of the goal and know what you must accomplish. You must accept the goal as something for which you are willing to work. It is important in setting and formulating goals to realize that you can consciously or unconsciously reject a goal (a) if you think it is too difficult, (b) if you think it is too easy, or (c) because you do not know what behaviors are needed for goal attainment. This understanding of goal-setting is critical to your success in using this method of self-motivation. Accepting the goal implies that you intend to engage in the behavior needed to achieve that goal.

It is also important for you to receive feedback about task performance. This guides you as to whether you should work harder, continue at the same pace, alter your approach or change your goal.

Striving for Results — A Self-Motivation Process

There are other theories that attempt to explain motivation and aid in our understanding of this important subject area. The design of this program, although it draws heavily on the GOAL-SETTING theory, is compatible and consistent with other theories, such as: *intrinsic motivation* — feelings of competence and self-control that come from performing enjoyable tasks, and *expectancy theory* — the relationship among desired outcomes, as they compare to the effort that one expends in carrying out their performance.

Let us review STRIVING FOR RESULTS from a motivational perspective. The first portion of the program enables you to construct, for yourself, a Goal-Setting Framework. This framework — consisting of a mission statement, vision, basic beliefs, and key result areas — enables you consciously to identify and express needs, drives, incentives and goals that you want to fulfill or achieve. It provides you with a means to articulate your interest in, attitudes toward, and purposes for your job/career. The exercises you used to generate your thoughts — like brainstorming, storywriting, and visualization — all draw upon the unconscious and conscious mental processes and information storage. Doing these activities in an evolving, developmental and reiterative (repeating the same task or tasks over and over) fashion helps you to refine your thinking, uncover and work through conflicts, and make choices based on updated information from both inside and outside yourself (other people, your immediate environment, etc.).

The SELF-MANAGEMENT PROCESS builds on the strong base you have created for yourself by providing you with a means to operationalize (put into action) the short-term goals required to achieve your long-term results. To be effective as a motivating force — that is, to energize you — you need to truly accept the goal, and you must know what behaviors are needed to attain your goal. At first glance, this may not appear very difficult. However, ask yourself this question: What do I have to do to improve in a particular task? A significant amount of analysis must go into answering such a question before you can construct a plan that you can actually put into action. I am sure you have already experienced this work through the exercises in this guide.

The benefits of developing a clear set of goals for yourself should be more and more apparent to you. Recall the benefits for you to consider:

GOALS:

-help you to CONCENTRATE

-add to your SELF-RESPECT

-create a SENSE OF PURPOSE and

       ANTICIPATION IN LIFE

-can help you to MAKE GOOD DECISIONS

-help you to SAVE TIME

-are great CONFIDENCE BUILDERS

-can REDUCE CONFLICT

Techniques for Self-Motivation

SELF-TALK — This is a way to assess the disposition of your attitude as "positive" or "negative." As if you were stepping outside yourself, observe what you say to yourself and evaluate whether it is positive or negative. Over a given period of time, say 20 to 30 minutes, how many responses were positive? How many were negative? This will give you an indication of your disposition.

POSITIVE AFFIRMATIONS — An affirmation is defined as the act of asserting or confirming as true. Some have called affirmations self-commands, self-suggestions, or self-talk. We can find many examples of affirmations in our everyday life, such as quotations, proverbs, sayings, and axioms like "Beauty is only skin deep" or "To have a friend, you must be a friend." Other examples of affirmations are marriage vows, oaths, pledges, and anthems. Basically, personal positive affirmation means saying good things about yourself: being conscious of and telling yourself what your strengths are or what you want them to be. Too often, we focus our attention on negative thoughts about ourselves and others in the world around us. The more prevalent these negative thoughts are in our minds, the more we will be prone to low self-image. In the computer world, there is a saying: Garbage in, garbage out; or Good stuff in, good stuff out.

Our attitude is programmed much like a computer. We have a choice and a responsibility in the programming of our thoughts and behaviors. To some extent, this programming begins at infancy or before when we have no control or influence over it. However, the older we get, the more influence and control we have. At this stage of your life, you may need or desire to modify what you have learned — that is, the way you have been conditioned or programmed. You can do this. This and other techniques can aid in the process of reconditioning yourself.

You can reinforce this positive conditioning process right now through a simple exercise. Over the next week, each morning or evening, write down one, two or possibly three positive affirmations about yourself. Write them on a small piece of paper. Put that piece of paper in your pocket and occasionally look at it throughout the day. This simple exercise of positively affirming yourself can contribute towards building self-confidence and fostering a positive self-image.

POSITIVE VISUALIZATION — We have a very powerful innate force: the ability to visualize. Through our imagination, we can create mental pictures of who we are and who we want to be, where we want to be and how. In my practice, I have sometimes used a projective technique to find out how people perceive themselves. It is a very simple exercise I ask a person to draw three pictures: (1) how others see them, (2) how they see themselves, and (3) the person they would like to be. It can be a revealing exercise. Begin to use this power in a creative and positive way.

SELF-DISCLOSURE — This is another powerful motivating force. Disclosing oneself to others whom you trust and respect can be a positive reinforcement, for you to live up to that disclosure and to achieve those goals. Sharing your desires, aspirations, and your goals with these people can provide outer support and encouragement and foster the inner desire to meet those expectations. This will be discussed more in the next chapter.

MIND MAPPING — This is a way to group your ideas and outline your thinking around a purpose or end result you want to achieve. It helps you to see the linkage between cause and effect. It helps you to organize your actions and direct your behavior.

AN EXAMPLE OF MIND MAPPING

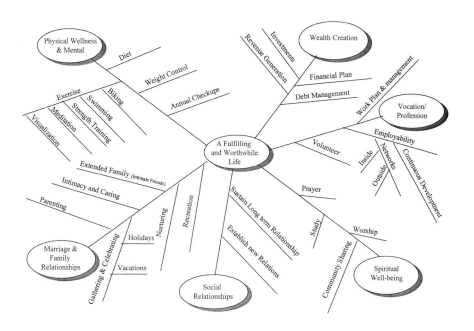

These simple techniques, along with the other tools provided, such as your goal-setting framework and self-management process, will provide you with effective means for self-motivation. In our next chapter, we will look at how you can further influence others to help you to succeed.

Personal Development Exercise #4:

Choose one of these techniques and practice it daily for fifteen minutes. In your workbook, record your impressions, however silly they might seem to you. Reread them at the end of the week, and see how much you learn. Record these impressions.

A WAY TO INFLUENCE OTHERS TO HELP YOU SUCCEED

Granted, as you build toward your dream, you will get tired. You will grow weary. You will need to stop and recharge. When those times come, you will need inspiration. Beyond inspiration, you will need great vision.

Dexter R. Yager, Sr.

For every disciplined effort there is a multiple reward.

Jim Rohn

EARLIER IN THESE CHAPTERS, I stressed the importance of having a clear direction, a sense of dedication and the ability to visualize what you want to achieve and accomplish (your Mission and Vision). I stated the importance of knowing the areas to focus on in expending your resources to achieve these desired results (Key Result Areas). I emphasized the importance of knowing your strengths and how to develop them, as well as your limitations or shortcomings and how to manage them or eliminate them through a well-planned and monitored development program (Self-Management Process). Included in this program would be the need to establish specific short-term realistic goals to ensure a sense of accomplishment, ongoing progress, and the joy and excitement that accompanies these successes.

Equally important to the above is the recognition and realization that much of what we do and accomplish is achieved through joint efforts with others. We complete less on our own than we do through mutual dependence or interdependence with others. Here are a few examples:

• A manager needs employees to be successful;

• An employee needs a manager who is successful;

• Both need a business or work unit within which to achieve their success;

• A business organization needs managers and employees, customers and suppliers.

There are many other interdependencies that exist between you, others, and your desired results. You will have an opportunity to discover these and understand them better in this chapter. You also will develop a better understanding of how you can positively influence or manage these important relationships.

Developing Trust - the Cornerstone to Effective Relationships

ONE OF THE KEY CHARACTERISTICS to a mutually satisfying and successful relationship is trust! In many consulting situations, I have been brought in to help resolve broken relationships or to help develop strong and effective relationships — restoring or building trust is always a goal. How do we go about building trust? Does it just happen because we want it? Or because we like our associates? Let us examine the model below for some of these answers.

TRUST MODEL
THE FOUNDATION OF RELATIONSHIPS

TRUST

OPENNESS

• Be Truthful
• Listen and Believe
• Admit Mistakes

CREDIBILITY

• Be Dependable
• Be Fair and Respectful

MAKING AND KEEPING AGREEMENTS

• Make Clear Agreements
• Set Achievable Goals

Look at the first building block, Making and Keeping Agreements. This begins with establishing a common purpose and mutual expectations for the relationship. We are referring to making and keeping commitments. If for some reason we cannot keep a commitment, we need to notify the other party. This leads directly to credibility, the ability to follow through, to do what we said we would do. Given that we don't live in a perfect world where we can predict all things, there is a need for openness of mind and spirit. A willingness to accept change; an appreciation for new information and circumstances.

Use this model to assess existing relationships and to make them more effective, to foster trust. Also use it as a guide for yourself to become more trustworthy in the eyes of others.

Stakeholder Relationships

THESE KEY RELATIONSHIPS I refer to as *Stakeholder Relationships*. The term stakeholder implies that there will be some benefit directly or indirectly, actually or potentially gained through this relationship. For instance, managers and employees have a mutual stakeholder relationship; so do parents and children, and husbands and wives. An example of an indirect stakeholder relationship would be your place of work and an individual employee.

The challenge in examining any of these relationships is to identify the mutual interdependencies that exist; that is, how does one benefit from the other — the "What's in it for me?" and "What's in it for them?" that makes this relationship important to both parties. How can we be mutually successful?

Personal Development Exercise #5:

IDENTIFYING KEY STAKEHOLDERS

Before trying to address these questions and others that I have just identified, let's first identify for ourselves who the key stakeholders are. I may have identified a few for you. Take a blank sheet in your workbook and draw a box, as indicated in the diagram below, putting yourself in the middle and extending a number of lines out from this box connecting to others.

Identify for yourself who some of your key stakeholders may be, such as boss, clients, co-workers, family, and others.

KEY STAKEHOLDERS

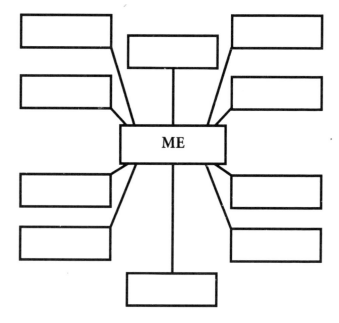

Have you forgotten any key stakeholders? Remember what I said earlier: you are a total person, and, as a total person, you carry out many significant roles in your life such as parent, spouse, worker, friend, or member of other organizations. Many of these roles are not separated from one another in terms of impact or influence. For instance, if you do not carry out your responsibilities as expected by your spouse, it is unlikely that he/she will look favorably towards you when you request his or her support in other activities. Can you see once again the importance of identifying the key result areas that contribute to your overall success and specific results? Do you see once again that in goal-setting it is important to be able to establish not only job-related goals, but also those that relate to key areas in your life outside of the job?

I know that much of what I am saying is not new to many of you. Over the years that I have worked with organizations and their employees, I have become readily aware that those who are successful in their jobs, in most instances, have been equally successful in other parts of their lives. Many of the skills you have learned through your career, such as good planning, self-discipline, and good organization, have contributed to your personal success in other parts of your lives. Also, both consciously and unconsciously, you have learned the importance of meeting other requirements and responsibilities outside of your job, so that you could and would be supported by others to accomplish what you want in your career.

Building Mutually Meaningful Relationships

You can look at any social relationship from two perspectives:

(1)   Its function or purpose, and

(2)   How it is executed or maintained.

Now, having identified your key stakeholder relationships, the next task that you have in building those relationships is to ask yourself, "Why do these relationships exist?" What are the expectations that each party has of themselves and the other? Are these expectations mutually clear to one another? The answers to these questions fall within the realm of the first dimension of social relationship — function or purpose. How are these expectations being met? Do both parties mutually support and contribute to each other's feelings of fulfillment and satisfaction from the relationship? These questions fall within the second dimension of social relationship — maintenance of the relationship.

Personal Development Exercise #6:
I D E N T I F Y I N G   A N D   R A T I N G   M U T U A L   E X P E C T A T I O N S

H E R E   I S   A N O T H E R   E X E R C I S E for you, as illustrated in the following diagram. In the left-hand column under WHO, write the name or position of the other party in the relationship, such as your manager, and his or her name. In the center of the page under the title EXPECTATIONS, you have two columns: in the left-hand column write down what

you think the other person's expectations are of the relationship, and in the corresponding column on the right, write
down your expectations of the relationship. The far right-
hand column is entitled RATING. Use a rating scale of 1 to 5,
with 1 being very low. A rating of 1 would indicate there are
not clear expectations within the relationship, conflict usually
exists, or there is evidence of lack of mutual support. A rating
of 5 would indicate clear and mutually understood expectations within the relationship, with evidence of mutual support
and respect for each other.

Who	Expectations		Rating (1-5)
	(Others)	(Mine)	

Now that you have identified the key stakeholders
affecting your success and rated the effectiveness of your
existing relationships, you should have a better sense of what
each relationships is, as you perceive it, and where you may
seek improvements.

Ways to Maintain and Improve Relationships

Here are some suggestions.

Express appreciation.

HOW OFTEN DO YOU EXPRESS your appreciation to others who support you in your activities? How many "thank yous" do you extend in a day? It's the little things that count. Others, like you, like to be appreciated for what they do. Just think how positively you respond to recognition!

Show interest in others' pursuits and accomplishments.

DO YOU KNOW WHAT IS IMPORTANT to others, such as friends, co-workers, your manager, and spouse? How much do you know about what they are doing? What is important to them? How often do you ask how their day was, give words of encouragement, or words of congratulations?

Be enthusiastic about your job/career/life.

ENTHUSIASM IS CONTAGIOUS. Communicate your excitement and interest in your career to others. Those who have an interest in you and care for you will support your enthusiasm and your positive attitude. They will identify with your aspirations and positive expectations. They will sense the meaningfulness of your endeavors to you. They will gravitate towards you and want to be a part of your success.

Another way of improving relationships is by using the information you generated above in your role expectation exercise with the other person in the relationship. Discuss how you see the relationship, that is, the mutual expectations and how you have rated them. This may sound a bit risky, however, it would actively demonstrate that you are interested in that relationship, that you value it, and that you would like to improve that relationship. Tell the person how you came about this exercise and how it relates to your interest in your career. Think of using it as an opportunity. Remember what I said earlier about "self-disclosure" and how you can use this as a means of self-motivation. This self-disclosure is also a powerful means to influence others to help you succeed.

Improving your Communication Skills

AS YOU CAN WELL IMAGINE BY NOW, a firm understanding of interpersonal communication and skill at communicating are effective means of influencing others to help you succeed. There are at least five essential ingredients found in effective interpersonal relationships. They are an ability to: (1) express empathy towards the other; (2) put yourself in their shoes; (3) express warmth and caring; (4) communicate a sense of genuineness; (5) be open and honest in your relationship with that person. Try to remember these ingredients when you're relating to others — expressing an interest in their lives in the same manner as you would like them to express an interest in yours. Keep in mind such expressions as: the importance of giving to receive; that a relationship needs to work two ways; the need for collaboration, understanding, and "giving in" to self and opening to our success. Take time to stop and rethink what is going on in your relationships with others.

ON YOUR JOURNEY
TOWARDS SUCCESS

There is an old story told about a Zen monk who walked across China. His disciples, awed at the accomplishment, asked him one day, "How did you do it?" The old monk was stymied at the query.

Finally, he asked his disciples, "How would you do it?" His greatest disciples had no answer. His lesser disciples had no answer. Finally, the youngest, simplest disciple, who almost never spoke, answered quietly, "One step at a time."

The old monk grinned and replied, "The journey of a thousand miles begins with a single step."

Zen Proverb

". . . success really comes with doing the little things right day after day."

Marty Schottenheimer
Head Coach, Kansas City Chiefs

"And will you succeed? Yes! You will (98 and 3/4 percent guaranteed.) Kid, you'll move mountains!"

Dr. Seuss

THIS IS THE KIND OF GUIDE that you can use over and over again throughout your life and career, either in part or in whole. Your vision of yourself and where you want to be and, of course, the means that you use to get there, will evolve and change over time.

Relationships with others will also change. You have to form new relationships. This is all part of a lifelong process. The concepts and exercises have broad application and, therefore, you can use them to help define all parts of your life, to assess current directions, and to chart new ones for yourself.

When you think of success for yourself, think of it in terms of the process you have just experienced. In fact, when you think of yourself, think of success! And apply the Five Basic Principles and Striving for Results.

You can think of SUCCESS as the following acronym:

S ense of Meaning, Purpose, and Vision

U nderstand yourself, others and the world

C ommitment

C ourage

E nthusiasm

S hare your Vision and Goals with others

S upport others in their Quest for Success!

Recently I came across a number of very successful people who not only fit the above acronym but who are affiliated with the same corporation. This corporation fosters an environment of positive mental conditioning that embodies the Five Basic Principles and provides a system that can duplicate this same level of performance over and over.

The common characteristics I identified in studying over forty people involved in this business were the following:

Changing lifestyle from surviving to fulfilling their dreams;

Creating financial freedom from indebtedness and feelings of financial insecurity;

Transforming themselves through helping others to be successful.

These three characteristics were supported by a fourth that I characterize as the foundation stone, Building Relationships. The dynamism I observed in these professionals is similar to what one may experience going through the process described in this book.

The symbol for marriage in Chinese aptly demonstrates this change process. While this traditional symbol represents marriage, the elements within it are universal and can apply to any relating we experience.

The background symbol is that of the yin-yang; it embraces the dragon and the phoenix. These three symbols reflect various characteristics of change. The yin-yang circle shows the pattern of continuous change — between night and day, death and rebirth, male and female — any polarity. This ancient symbol reveals how the dynamic tension between opposites creates change.

I am sure that we are able to identify many of these tensions in contemporary life today. The challenge is to be in harmony with the inevitable cycle of change and, to do this, one must learn to move gracefully between polarities.

The dragon is the more active agent of change. It creates transformation by breathing the fire of both creativity and destruction. It represents eternal change and the need to be continuously creative, innovative and adaptive. Its usually red color symbolizes both vitality and transformation, the purifying effect of the refiner's fire.

The symbol of the dragon is apropos and exemplifies the transforming behaviors that are fostered in **Inspiration at Work:** goal-setting, self-discipline, self-motivation, self-study, giving and loving, and sacrifice.

The phoenix appears in many cultures as a symbol of change through renewal. It rises on wings of flame from the ashes of its former self. This mythological bird offers hope in the spirit of rising above destruction, transcending loss, and recreating ourselves and our organizations.

This spirit of hope is not only applicable, it is critical to the success of any individual in the corporate world today. We all need to rise above whatever destruction is going on around us, despite our fears. We also have to transcend the sense of loss that we experience in letting go of the old and taking on the new.

Both the dragon and the phoenix are associated with fire. The dragon breathes fire and the phoenix is transformed through fire. When organizations go through large scale change, the impact on both individuals and systems can be like emerging from a fire. Many of us who are working in large corporations have felt the devastating, yet transforming, effects of the changes that have gone on and are going on within the corporate world in recent years. Will we be the dragon who creates the change? Will we be the phoenix who transcends the fire? Will we be both?

The dragon and the phoenix work together representing eternal change and creative renewal. It is through the combination of the two that we make progress, for renewal without change is illusion, and change without renewal is chaos.

BIBLIOGRAPHY

Entrepreneurial Development

Brant, Steven C. **ENTREPRENEURING IN ESTABLISHED COMPANIES.** Dow Jones-Irwin, 1986.

Cullinane, John J. **THE ENTREPRENEUR'S SURVIVAL GUIDE: 101 Tips for Managing in Good Times & Bad.** Richard D. Irwin, 1993.

Drucker, Peter F. **INNOVATION AND ENTREPRENEUR-SHIP: Practice and Principles.** Harper & Row, Publishers, 1985.

Drucker, Peter F. **THE NEW REALITIES.** Harper & Row, Publishers, 1989.

Kanter, Rosabeth Moss. **THE CHANGE MASTERS: Innovation and Entrepreneurship in the American Corporation.** Simon & Schuster, 1983.

McQuown, Judith H. **INC. YOURSELF: How To Profit By Setting Up Your Own Corporation.** Harper Business, 1995.

Tomasko, Robert M. **GO FOR GROWTH: Five Paths to Profit and Success — Choose the Right One for You and Your Company.** John Wiley & Sons, Inc., 1996.

Yager, Dexter. **MILLIONAIRE MENTALITY: Financial Freedom Can Be Yours.** InterNET Services, 1993.

Organization Development

Ackoff, Russel L. **THE DEMOCRATIC CORPORATION: A Radical Presentation for Recreating Corporate America and Rediscovering Success.** Oxford University Press, 1994.

Canfield, Jack and Jacqueline Miller. **HEART AT WORK.** McGraw-Hill, 1996.

Collier, Lindsay. **WHACK-A-MOLE THEORY: Creating Breakthrough and Transformation in Organizations.** WhAM Books, 1996.

Covey, Stephen R. **PRINCIPLE-CENTERED LEADERSHIP.** Simon & Schuster, 1991.

McCall, Morgan W., Michael M. Lomardo and Ann M. Morrison. **THE LESSONS OF EXPERIENCE: How Successful Executives Develop on the Job.** Lexington Books, 1988.

Peters, Tom. **THRIVING ON CHAOS: Handbook for a Management Revolution.** Harper & Row, 1987.

Richardson, Barrie. **THE PLUS 10 PERCENT PRINCIPLE: How to Get Extraordinary Results from Ordinary People.** Pfeiffer & Company, 1993.

Senge, Peter M. **THE FIFTH DISCIPLINE: The Art & Practice of The Learning Organization.** Doubleday Currency, 1990.

Senge, Peter M. et.al. THE FIFTH DISCIPLINE FIELD-BOOK: Strategies and Tools for Building a Learning Organization. Doubleday Currency, 1994.

Tomasko, Robert M. RETHINKING THE CORPORA-TION: The Architecture of Change. AMACOM, 1993.

Mental Conditioning

Butler, Gillian and Tony Hope. MANAGING YOUR MIND: The Mental Fitness Guide. Oxford University Press, 1995.

Covey, Stephen R. THE SEVEN HABITS OF HIGHLY EFFECTIVE PEOPLE. Simon & Schuster, 1989.

Covey, Stephen R., Roger Merrill and Rebecca R. Merrill. FIRST THINGS FIRST. Simon & Schuster, 1994.

Garfield, Charles A. PEAK PERFORMANCE: Mental Training Techniques of the World's Greatest Athletes. Warner Books, Inc., 1985.

Gawain, Shakti. CREATIVE VISUALIZATION. New World Library, 1995.

Gelb, Michael J. THINKING FOR A CHANGE: Discovering the Power to Create, Communicate, and Lead. Harmony Books, 1995.

Kriegel, Robert and Marilyn Harris Kriegel. THE C ZONE: Peak Performance Under Pressure. Anchor Press/Doubleday, 1984.

Tichy, Noel M. and Stratford Sherman. CONTROL YOUR DESTINY OR SOMEONE ELSE WILL. Doubleday, 1993.

Waitley, Denis. THE NEW DYNAMICS OF WINNING. William Morrow and Company, 1993.

Waitley, Denis. EMPIRES OF THE MIND. William Morrow and Company, 1995.

Spiritual Development

Chopra, Deepak. THE SEVEN SPIRITUAL LAWS OF SUCCESS. Amber-Allen, 1994.

Chopra, Deepak. THE WAY OF THE WIZARD: Twenty Spiritual Lessons for Creating the Life You Want. Harmony Books, 1995.

Corso, Susan. THE PEACE DIET: The 44 Day Feast to Personal Peace. Dona Nobis Pacem Press, 1996.

Hanh, Thich Nhat. PEACE IS EVERY STEP: The Path of Mindfulness in Everyday Life. Bantam Books, 1991.

Jones, Laurie Beth. JESUS CEO: USING ANCIENT WISDOM FOR VISIONARY LEADERSHIP. Hyperion, 1995.

AUTHOR PROFILE

DR. BOB RUOTOLO has over thirty years of Organization Development and Corporate Human Resources management and consulting experience. Formerly President of Performance Management Consulting, a firm providing services and products in career and performance management systems, business process reengineering, and total quality management implementation, Bob's talents are now focused on AlliedSignal Aerospace.

An internal consultant for Allied, Bob designs and implements large-scale change efforts for management and staff. In addition, he continues to travel and consult privately with businesses, corporations, and not-for-profit organizations. His workshops, speeches, and seminars meet with critical accolades. He has worked with Olympic athletes to reach peak performance through mental conditioning. He had a clinical social work practice for fifteen years.

Some of his corporate clients include: Exxon USA, Imperial Oil Ltd. - Canada, Government of Bermuda, Bank of New South Wales - Australia, and the Petroleum Association for the Conservation of Canadian Environment; as well as numerous not-for-profits, educational and professional organizations.

Bob has been married to Patricia for thirty years. They have three daughters, Kymberly, Kara-Lee and Kinsey-Beth. He lives in the Ahwatukee foothills in Phoenix, Arizona.

How To Reach The Author

Dr. Bob Ruotolo welcomes your feedback, stories and comments. Please write to him:

3941 East Chandler Blvd., Suite 209
Phoenix, AZ 85044
602/407-8155
Fax 602/759-0889

He is available by invitation to present seminars, workshops and speeches for your corporation, organization, downline, educational institution, professional group, or company. Consulting services are also possible. Please feel free to contact him and explore the options.

602/407-8155

INSPIRATION AT WORK

CATALOG
OF
PRODUCTS

DR. ROBERT A. RUOTOLO
3941 East Chandler Blvd., Suite 209
Phoenix, AZ 85044
602/407-8155 Fax 602/759-0889

Order Form

Yes, I want to take a leap forward in my career! I am ordering the following products:

Inspiration At Work
_____   Book(s) @ $14.95   _____

Striving For Results
_____   Workbook(s) @ $39.95   _____

Striving For Results (4 audiotapes)
Topics include:
- A Way To Achieve Your Goals
- An Approach to Self-Management
- A Way To Influence Others To Help you Succeed
- Managing Stress & Improving Performance
- Creating New Mental Software & Power of Affirmation
- The Journey to S.U.C.C.E.S.S.
- The Power of Mental Conditioning: A Coaching Guide to Improving
  Performance & Employee Satisfaction
_____   Audiotape Set(s) @ $59.95   _____
Save!
_____   Workbook/Tape Set(s) @ $90.00   _____

Send To_____   Subtotal   _____

Address_____   Shipping   _____

City/State/Zip_____   Tax   _____

Day Phone _____   Total   _____

Please enclose Money Order or Check to: **Dr. Robert A. Ruotolo.**
Sales Tax: Please add 7.6% for items shipped to Arizona addresses.
Shipping: If your order totals:

$00.00 - $24.99	= $4.00
$25.00 - $49.99	= $7.00
$50.00 - $74.99	= $11.00
$75.00 and up	= 15% of total

INSPIRATION AT WORK

CATALOG
OF
PRODUCTS

DR. ROBERT A. RUOTOLO
3941 East Chandler Blvd., Suite 209
Phoenix, AZ 85044
602/407-8155   Fax 602/759-0889

Order Form

Yes, I want to take a leap forward in my career! I am ordering the following products:

Inspiration At Work
_____   Book(s) @ $14.95   _____

Striving For Results
_____   Workbook(s) @ $39.95   _____

Striving For Results (4 audiotapes)
Topics include:
- A Way To Achieve Your Goals
- An Approach to Self-Management
- A Way To Influence Others To Help you Succeed
- Managing Stress & Improving Performance
- Creating New Mental Software & Power of Affirmation
- The Journey to S.U.C.C.E.S.S.
- The Power of Mental Conditioning: A Coaching Guide to Improving
  Performance & Employee Satisfaction
_____   Audiotape Set(s) @ $59.95   _____

Save!
_____   Workbook/Tape Set(s) @ $90.00   _____

Send To_____   Subtotal   _____

Address_____   Shipping   _____

City/State/Zip_____   Tax   _____

Day Phone _____   Total   _____

Please enclose Money Order or Check to: **Dr. Robert A. Ruotolo.**
Sales Tax: Please add 7.6% for items shipped to Arizona addresses.
Shipping: If your order totals:
        $00.00 - $24.99   = $4.00
        $25.00 - $49.99   = $7.00
        $50.00 - $74.99   = $11.00
        $75.00 and up   = 15% of total